W9-ARI-926

—Diseases and People—

PYROMANIA, KLEPTOMANIA, AND OTHER IMPULSE-CONTROL DISORDERS

Julie Williams

Enslow Publishers, Inc.

40 Industrial Road	PO Box 38
Box 398	Aldershot
Berkeley Heights, NJ 07922	Hants GU12 6BP
USA	UK

http://www.enslow.com

For Ian

Library of Congress Cataloging-in-Publication Data

Williams, Julie, 1954-
   Pyromania, kleptomania, and other impulse control disorders. / Julie Williams.
      p. cm. — (Diseases and people)
   Includes bibliographical references and index. Summary: Describes the characteristics
of impulsive-control disorders, their possible genetic, developmental, and chemical
causes, related disorders, and treatments.
      ISBN 0-7660-1899-7
      1. Impulse-control disorders—Juvenile literature. [1. Impulse-control disorders.]
I. Title. II. Series.
      RC569.5.I46 W54 2002
      616.85'84—dc21
      2001005945

Printed in the United States of America

10 9 8 7 6 5 4 3 2

To Our Readers:
We have done our best to make sure all Internet Addresses in this book were active and
appropriate when we went to press. However, the author and the publisher have no control
over and assume no liability for the material available on those Internet sites or on other Web
sites they may link to. Any comments or suggestions can be sent by e-mail to
comments@enslow.com or to the address on the back cover.

Illustration Credits: Archiv Pierre et Marie Curie, p. 10; Associated Press/Cesar
Rangel, p. 73; Associated Press/Matt York, p. 65; Associated Press/Robie Family via
Corning Leader, p. 77; Associated Press/Scott Audette, p. 90; © Corel
Corporation, pp. 14, 34, 36, 49, 58, 62, 79, 85, 96; Courtesy of Craig Hospital,
Englewood, Colorado. p. 24; Courtesy of Photofest, Inc., p. 42; Courtesy of the
National Library of Medicine, pp. 19, 21, 23; Enslow Publishers, Inc., p. 9;
National Institute of Neurological Disorders and Stroke, p. 101; William Sauts
Bock, p. 18.

Cover Illustration: Corbis Images Royalty-Free (main); Enslow Publishers, Inc. (inset).

Contents

PYROMANIA, KLEPTOMANIA,
AND OTHER IMPULSE-CONTROL
DISORDERS

What are Impulse-Control Disorders? Impulse-control disorders (ICDs) involve the repeated inability to resist doing something harmful to oneself or to others. There are five specific disorders: pyromania, kleptomania, trichotillomania, pathological gambling, and intermittent explosive disorder.

Who gets them? People of both sexes and all races can have one or more ICDs. Women are more likely than men to suffer from trichotillomania or kleptomania. Men experience intermittent explosive disorder, gambling, and pyromania more often than women do. All these disorders can appear in children or adolescents.

What are the causes? The causes of most cases of ICD are unknown. A tendency toward an ICD may be inherited. Head injuries are associated with a loss of impulse control.

What are the symptoms? Repeated impulsive acts that cause harm to the person or to others. The kind of action determines which specific ICD the person suffers from. For example, if a person steals things he or she does not need, the ICD is identified as kleptomania. Many people have more than one ICD, or experience a series of ICDs.

How are they treated? Behavioral and cognitive therapy is usually tried first. Some people respond to medications, but the effect of medication is unpredictable. An impulsive act leading to a crime may result in arrest and jail time.

How can they be prevented? Early identification and counseling of impulsive children and their families is one of the best, but most challenging, ways to prevent ICD. The behavior seen in destructive impulsive actions constitutes a nationwide social problem that is becoming more serious.

1

What are Impulse-Control Disorders?

Josh Sneed was a slightly built high school freshman from Powell, Tennessee. His family was not as sophisticated or as wealthy as some others. A group of boys found him an easy target to tease. For three months, Josh tried to ignore them. Then, the teasing turned to threats of violence. One day, Josh said he "just snapped." As one of his tormentors passed him in the cafeteria line, Josh hit him with a tray and started punching him. The other boy hit back.

Josh now has four titanium plates holding his skull together. The other student was not hurt badly, but was suspended from school for 133 days.[1]

Nine-year-old Jessica liked to make a wish every time one of her eyelashes fell out. It was a family custom. She started pulling her eyelashes out on purpose, so she could make more wishes. When her eyelashes were gone, she started on her eyebrows. Her mother became worried about her hair loss and took her to a doctor. The doctor suggested therapy, which Jessica refused. She stopped the hair pulling a few months later.

Two years later, she started pulling the hair from her head. When she returned from summer camp, her mother was shocked to see that she was completely bald. Therapy and medication did not help. Finally, Jessica refused any more treatment and wore a wig. Kids at school teased her and even tried to pull her wig off. After several years of misery, she was again able to stop pulling her hair on her own.

When she began pulling her hair out for the third time, Jessica accepted medication for a few months. The medication helped her to stop pulling. This time, when the medications ended, she did not start pulling her hair again.

Jessica knows that the urge to pull her hair may return. She knows she will have to seek treatment again for a disorder whose cause is unknown, and for which no cure exists.[2]

Both Josh and Jessica were unable to control their impulses. Both suffered serious consequences because of their lack of control.

What is an Impulse?

An impulse is a sudden feeling or urge to act that arises in a person's mind. It is not a conscious plan or desire. It is not a suggestion from someone else. Acting on a sudden feeling is called an impulsive action. The habit of acting without thinking more frequently than others of the same knowledge and ability is called impulsivity. [3]

Everyone experiences impulses, and all of us act without thinking from time to time. When we feel an impulse to do something, we have several choices. We can go ahead and act

Following a Hunch

"Following a hunch," another word for an impulsive idea, has helped countless scientists find solutions for difficult problems. The Rosetta Stone is slab of black basalt (which is solidified volcanic lava) from Egypt, inscribed with the same message in three different languages. Greek and the ancient Egyptian pictorial script called hieroglyphics were two of these languages. Napoleon's soldiers discovered the stone as they were retreating from their attempted invasion of Egypt in 1799.

Scholars easily translated the Greek text, but the strange symbols of the ancient Egyptian hieroglyphics remained a tantalizing secret. In 1821, the Frenchman Jean François Champollion (1790–1832) was spending his birthday studying the Egyptian and Greek words inscribed on the famous monument. Impulsively, he began comparing the Egyptian symbols and the Greek words. He had a hunch that the Egyptian symbols represented syllables, or parts of words, and not complete words. This idea went completely against the beliefs of other scholars. Champollion's impulsive comparison of the scripts on the stone proved to be correct, and a complete understanding of the long-forgotten Egyptian script soon followed.

The famous scientist Marie Curie (1867–1934), winner of two Nobel Prizes, is well known for her discovery of radium, a natural metallic element that emits radioactivity as it decays. This discovery took many years of disciplined work and paved the way for radiation treatments for skin disorders and cancer. But her greatest contribution to science was her intuition that radioactivity arises from radium atoms. It does not depend on an outside source of energy. In her day, scientists thought that the sun provided all electrical energy and light. No one thought to look into the center of matter itself. Marie Curie's insight unlocked the awesome power of atomic energy in the twentieth century.[4]

However, impulsive ideas have a down side when they lead to harmful actions. If you see a CD in the store and buy it instead of getting the groceries that your family needs, your spontaneous decision will cost your family their meal. If you steal the CD instead of paying for it, the consequences will be even worse.

Marie Curie's intuition that radioactivity arises from radium atoms was one of the greatest scientific contributions ever made.

immediately. We can think about what we are going to do, and deliberately choose to act. We can change what we plan to do based on how we think it will turn out, or how it will affect others, or what is going on around us at the moment. Finally, we can choose not to act at all. It is all up to us.

Intuitions, hunches, and insights are all forms of impulsive thoughts. When you spontaneously hug a friend after she tells you that her cat was run over by a car, you are acting in an impulsive yet positive way. Impulsive people bubble with high energy and new ideas. They often appear brave and spontaneous. The bumper sticker urging us to "Commit random acts of senseless kindness" was probably created by an impulsive person.

Definition of Impulse-Control Disorders

A person is said to suffer from an impulse-control disorder when he or she is unable to resist "an impulse, drive, or temptation to perform an act that is harmful to the person or to others." Usually "the individual feels an increasing sense of tension or arousal before committing the act and then experiences pleasure, gratification, or relief at the time of committing the act. Following the act there may or may not be regret, self-reproach, or guilt."

This definition comes from the *Diagnostic and Statistical Manual of Mental Disorders,* Fourth Edition, Text Revision (DSM-IV-TR), a reference book written by psychiatrists and psychologists. The DSM-IV identifies five specific Impulse-Control Disorders (ICDs):

- kleptomania (stealing objects one does not need)

- pyromania (setting fires for pleasure)

- pathological gambling

- trichotillomania (pulling one's hair out)

- intermittent explosive disorder (episodes of aggression that harm other people or property)

The DSM-IV-TR calls these five disorders "Not Elsewhere Classified," and lists them separately because they do not fit in with any other types of disorders discussed in the manual. However, problems with impulse control commonly occur as part of many psychological disorders. Drug and alcohol abuse, eating disorders, anxiety, and depression all contain elements of impulsivity. Persons suffering from disorders such as autism (not relating to others), mental retardation, schizophrenia (separation of thoughts and feelings), attention-deficit/hyperactivity disorder, obsessive-compulsive disorder (experiencing upsetting thoughts and following ritual behaviors to try to control them), and some personality disorders (repeated patterns of socially unacceptable behavior) may also have trouble controlling their impulses. These disorders, and the impulsivity that accompanies them, appear to arise from many different causes. According to one estimate, half of all psychotherapy involves treatment for some kind of impulsive behavior.[5]

Understanding the Many Aspects of Impulsivity

We know that we all act impulsively from time to time and in different situations. Some of us do things spontaneously every once in a while. Usually, these off-the-cuff actions do not cause problems, and may even bring positive results. This type of impulsivity is called transient, meaning that it does not last long and it is not repeated frequently.

Repeated impulsive acts usually bring negative consequences. This type of impulsivity is defined as persistent, meaning that it is long-lasting and repeated.[6]

It is difficult to draw a line between occasional impulsive acts and an impulse-control disorder when both result in negative consequences. Feeling tired or bored, being irritated or aggressive, or just looking for some excitement can all make it harder for a person to handle his or her impulses. Experts do not agree on how to diagnose impulse-control problems in every situation. However, all agree that uncontrollable impulsive behaviors can cause severe problems at home, at school, and at work.

Stages of Impulsive Behavior

Impulse-control problems generally occur at one of three points in an action:

1. The preparation stage, when a person acts before having all necessary information.

2. The execution stage, when a person does not follow instructions or interrupts during the action itself.

3. The outcome stage, when a person acts before determining the best outcome.[7]

Here are some examples. At which stage of acting impulsively does the impulse control problem occur?

*   A couple goes on vacation without making hotel reservations, and does not take enough money.

*   Children at a birthday party get into a fight because they cannot wait for their turns during the games.

*   A reader peeks at the ending of a mystery novel. He puts the book down because the plot is no longer interesting.

*   A woman gets lost because she does not listen to directions. Then, she drives too fast because she is late.

*   At the last minute, a boy decides to wear his oldest jeans to his grandparents' fiftieth anniversary celebration at their country club.

Development of Impulse Control

Children are born with little control over their impulses. The minute a baby is hungry, he cries. When a toddler wants a toy, she grabs for it. The ability to manage impulses, by acting on positive urges and filtering out or redirecting negative ones, normally increases as a person grows from childhood to adulthood. When this growth does not occur, impulses may become uncontrollable and even destructive. Impulse-control disorders are usually noticed first in childhood or adolescence. Research indicates that the number of adolescents exhibiting a lack of control over their behavior is growing.[8]

Children have little control over their impulses, but as they grow older, the ability to manage impulses increases.

Who Has An Impulse-Control Disorder?

It is very difficult to estimate the number of people who suffer from impulse-control disorders. People hesitate to identify themselves or seek help because they are ashamed of their behavior. Some impulsive acts, such as stealing and setting fire to buildings, are illegal. Many people only discover that they have an impulse-control disorder when they are arrested for a crime. The best estimates suggest that 1–3 percent of the general population, in all countries around the world, suffer from some type of these disorders.[9] Fewer than 5 percent of shoplifters are thought to suffer from kleptomania.[10] Pathological gambling afflicts up to 7 percent of people at some time in their lives.[11]

Slightly more women than men appear to be affected, although this ratio may be due to the fact that women are more likely to ask for help with problem behavior than men are. More women than men suffer from kleptomania and trichotillomania. Men are more likely to experience intermittent explosive disorder, compulsive gambling, and pyromania.[12] Many people struggle with more than one ICD.

A person with an ICD is not constantly out of control. Impulsive behavior usually occurs in episodes. There may be long periods of time, called remission, when the behavior seems to stop. A person may try different methods to control the impulsive behavior and the unhappiness it causes. Sometimes, repeated attempts at control become compulsive, meaning that they are irrationally carried out again and again. Such attempts at control rarely work, and leave the person with further distress.

It is not uncommon for a person to learn to control one impulsive habit, only to find that another habit has popped up in its place. For example, a woman might successfully stop shoplifting but find that she is beginning to pull her eyebrows out. These are called rotating impulsive behaviors, or symptom substitution.

Doctors and researchers are exploring causes and treatments of impulse-control disorders. Genetic, biological, and environmental factors all play roles in impulsivity.

2

History, Causes, and Treatment of Impulse-Control Disorders

mpulse-control disorders, along with many other psychological conditions, are doubtless as old as humanity. Stories from many ancient civilizations show the devastating results impulsive behavior can have.

A set of cuneiform tablets inscribed before 2000 B.C. tells the story of King Gilgamesh of Mesopotamia. Gilgamesh indulged his every impulse, fighting with men and chasing women, creating such havoc in his own kingdom that, it was said, the gods were forced to take action to stop him.

In chapter four of *Genesis*, Cain was overwhelmed by jealousy when his offering was rejected by God, and impulsively killed his brother, Abel. He was driven out of his home and bitterly regretted his action.

The plot of the first Greek epic, the *Iliad* (c. 750 B.C.), was set in motion by a series of impulsive, angry actions. Achilles, the

The mythological Greek hero, Achilles, suffered great consequences due to his impulsive decision to withdraw from a battle.

greatest hero of the Greeks, had received a female slave as a reward for his valor in battle. He quarreled with the leader of the Greeks, King Agamemnon, who became angry and impulsively took the woman away. Achilles, too, became angry and immediately withdrew from battle. His action soon cost the life of his best friend, who took his place in the war.

The Greek doctor Hippocrates (c.460–377 B.C.) believed that impulsive behavior was caused by yellow bile, a bodily fluid that the Greeks thought existed in a person's body. Too much of this substance made a person excitable and impulsive. Greek scientists and doctors felt that impulsivity was an important part of the human personality.

Impulsive behavior received little attention after the decline of classical Greek civilization. From approximately A.D. 400 to

1600 in Western Europe, impulsive thoughts and actions were attributed to the prompting of the devil. Impulses were considered signs of a bad, or immoral, character. The German Protestant Reformation leader Martin Luther (1483–1546) warned his flock to avoid impulses, which led to immorality and drunkenness. Little scientific research or philosophical inquiry into these urges was conducted during this time.

In 1801, the French doctor Philippe Pinel (1745–1826) wrote a medical-philosophical study of mental conditions. He noted that some individuals had no control over their impulsive acts. Some of his patients, despite being mentally stable,

Dr. Philippe Pinel, unlike other doctors of his time, did not believe that his impulsive patients were morally defective.

repeatedly did things that caused them great harm. They seemed unable to learn how to behave from the results of their actions. Unlike most other doctors of his time, Dr. Pinel did not condemn his impulsive patients as morally defective. He felt that their impulsive behavior was an illness of some kind.[1]

The New York doctor George Miller Beard published a book on nervous exhaustion in 1869. This complaint, fashionable at the time, was thought to be caused by the extraordinary pace of "modern" civilization. Doctors claimed that busy growing cities, the lightning speed of train transportation and communication by telegraph, along with heavier educational expectations for children, were all placing unbearable demands on the human nervous system. One of the symptoms of nervous exhaustion, which Dr. Beard called *neurasthenia,* was being overwhelmed by sudden emotions, such as joy, exhaustion, or rage. Dr. Beard felt that neurasthenia originated in the brain and spinal cord. Others noted that this ailment, dubbed "Dr. Beard's malady," seemed to run in families.[2]

The German psychiatrist Ehrlheim Hirt (1849–1922) published the first textbook to use the term "impulsive" not in an abstract sense, but as a description of specific symptoms a psychiatrist might observe in his or her own patients. In 1902, he described an impulsive personality as excitable, enthusiastic, and unreliable. He noted that an impulsive person could be cranky, angry, and loud, and was likely to have an explosive temper and to ignore the needs of other people.

After Hirt's time, all psychologists and psychiatrists have included impulsivity in their theories of human personality and behavior. Dr. Sigmund Freud (1856–1939), the founder of modern psychological practice, said that impulses were thoughts from the subconscious part of the mind, the part of which we are not

Dr. Sigmund Freud believed that everyone experienced impulses, and he stated that the impulses themselves were neither good nor bad.

aware. They broke through to consciousness when the rational part of our mind was not able to censor them. He felt that impulses were experienced by everyone, and declared that they were neither bad nor good. He thought they were linked to a person's biological makeup. In saying this, Freud helped people see that impulses themselves were universal and morally neutral.

The first edition of the *Diagnostic and Statistical Manual: Mental Disorders* (DSM-I), containing a description of all known mental and psychological disorders, appeared in 1952. Impulse-control disorders were not included until the third edition, in 1980. Trichotillomania did not appear until the revision of the third edition, in 1987. All five disorders appear in the fourth edition, published in 1994.

Causes

Many factors lie behind impulsive behavior and its positive or negative results. Some of the most important are the structure and chemical makeup of the brain, genetically inherited traits, and the person's family and immediate environment. Scientists are looking into all of these areas as they seek to learn more about and develop treatments for impulse-control disorders.

Structure of the Brain

The brain is the communication center of the human body. A human brain weighs about three pounds and has three main sections: the cerebrum, cerebellum, and the brain stem. The organs of the limbic system, a primitive part of the brain humans have in common with other mammals, lie beneath the cerebrum. The cerebrum, the cerebellum, and the limbic system all interact in producing and regulating emotions, impulses, and behavior.

The cerebrum is the biggest part of the human brain, making up approximately 85 percent of the whole organ. The cerebrum is proportionally larger in humans than in any other mammal. This gray, wrinkled mass sits on top of the rest of the brain and houses the faculties of human speech, memory, and thought. The cerebrum is divided into sections called lobes. Doctors in the early 1800s noticed that patients who suffered accidental damage to the two frontal lobes of the brain, located directly behind the forehead, often developed impulsive behavior patterns.[3] Recent research has revealed that this part of the cerebrum plays an important role in thinking ahead, learning from experience, and controlling behavior.

The cerebellum lies toward the back of the skull, beneath the cerebrum. It is a small, rounded mass of tissue the size of a child's fist, accounting for 10 percent of the total brain. It controls movement and coordination by connecting nerve impulses from the spinal cord to input from the frontal lobes. The cerebellum is also involved in what scientists call motor impulsivity. This term

Phineas Gage

Phineas Gage was a twenty-five-year-old construction foreman for the Rutland and Burlington Railroad in New England in 1848. Everyone thought he was an intelligent, responsible, and reliable young man. His many promotions foretold a bright future.

On September 13 of that year, he was the victim of a terrible and bizarre accident. He was supervising a group of men preparing a site for blasting out rocks in order to lay new railroad tracks. Without warning, the explosives ignited and a heavy metal rod was hurled directly toward Gage's head. It flew cleanly through his face and out the top of his skull. Gage lost consciousness, but was able to walk and talk almost immediately after the accident, to the astonishment of his doctor. His physical injuries healed quickly, and his memory and reasoning were not affected.

However, the incident had a more profound result. Gage suffered a major personality change. Instead of the serious, reliable citizen he was before, he lost all sense of responsibility. His actions were impulsive, unpredictable, and often offensive to those around him. His friends were shocked when Gage began swearing constantly.

He was soon fired from his job because his employers could no longer trust him to complete his work. Practically unemployable, he wandered around the United States, dying in poverty twelve years after the accident.[4]

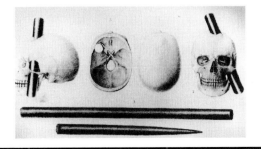

is used to describe physical activities that are inappropriate or not well-planned.

The various organs of the limbic system lie beneath the cerebrum, deep inside the skull. Like the cerebellum, the limbic system also connects to the spinal cord. This part of the brain generates the basic appetites and impulses connected with survival. Feelings of hunger, thirst, fear, sleep or wakefulness, sexuality, and other powerful emotions are aroused and registered here. Impulsive behaviors associated with feeling physically uncomfortable also arise from this part of the brain. So when you

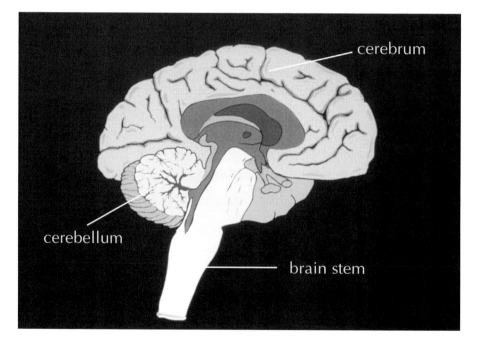

The cerebellum controls movement and coordination. The cerebrum generates basic impulses connected with hunger, thirst, sleep or wakefulness, and sexuality. The brain stem carries impulses from the cerebellum and cerebrum to the spinal cord.

wake up in the morning with a stiff neck and find yourself snapping at your family, you can blame your limbic system!

Each part of the brain—the frontal lobes, cerebellum, and the limbic system—is in constant contact with the others. The overall type, intensity, and frequency of impulsive behaviors appear to be the result of the interaction of all three parts. Poor communication among the different parts, rather than an abnormality in any one area, may be responsible for some kinds of impulsivity. [5]

Chemical Communication in the Brain

The brain contains billions of special cells called neurons. Their function is to transmit feelings, thoughts, and information. These cells look a bit like trees, with branches at one end and roots at the other, and a round center called the nucleus somewhere in the middle.

Neurons do not need to touch each other in order to send information. Instead, transmitters at one end of a neuron send special chemicals, called neurotransmitters, across the space to the next neuron. This space is called a synapse. Receptors located at the end of the next neuron receive the chemical information and pass it on.

This information transfer system is a complicated process. The information signal within the cell is electrical in nature. It must be converted to a chemical at the sending end of the neuron in order to move on. Then, the neuron must produce exactly the right amount of the neurotransmitter chemical. After the chemical signal passes through the synapse, the receptors at the end of the next neuron must be awake and ready to receive the signal. It is then converted back to electricity within the neuron. As an example of how complex the system is, scientists have identified at least fourteen different types of receptors for just one of the neurochemicals.[6]

Three brain chemicals, serotonin, norepinephrine, and dopamine, appear to affect a person's control of emotions and judgment. By studying the chemical makeup of patients' spinal fluid, doctors have found lower-than-normal levels of serotonin in the brains of many people with both impulsive and aggressive behavior problems. They have also found higher-than-normal levels of norepinephrine or dopamine in some people with impulsive behavior.[7]

However, an abnormal amount of one neurotransmitter, either low or high, does not always create a problem with impulse control. The way the three neurochemical systems interact appears to be critical. The wrong level of one chemical may stimulate over- or under-production of another chemical, and the imbalance results in impulsivity.[8] Many other biochemical

Three Neurotransmitters

- *Serotonin*: involved in handling feelings, emotions, and judgment.

- *Dopamine*: associated with feelings of excitement and pleasure. The overproduction of dopamine that occurs when certain drugs, alcohol or food is consumed may be responsible for addiction.

- *Norepinephrine*: stimulates the nervous system and releases energy.

systems in the body, such as hormones, also affect impulsive behavior.

Genetic Influences

Other important discoveries concerning the causes of impulsive behavior are being made in the field of genetic research. Genes are pieces of chromosomes, the blueprints our cells carry that create our basic characteristics. For example, a specific gene directs certain cells in the body to make our eyes a certain color. Some genes produce brown, some blue, and some green.

A single gene by itself does not usually determine one characteristic. One trait can be determined by many genes. The human body contains between 50,000 and 100,000 genes. Genes regularly interact with each other, creating multi-step paths to the final outcomes. This is especially true with complex traits such as behavior.

Doctors have long noted that a tendency to act impulsively appears to run in families. Several genes associated with specific human behavioral patterns have been discovered, providing physical evidence for this tendency. A gene associated with poor absorption of serotonin has been found in the chromosomes of some people who act both impulsively and aggressively. Other research has identified genes responsible for making abnormal levels of dopamine in impulsive people.

We must remember, however, that a genetic tendency is just a nudge in one direction, and not a shove.[9] Many other biological factors such as hormones, diet, and overall health have a significant impact on a person's behavior. If we think of a person's genetic background as being like a roadmap, we know that the actual journey a person takes in life is influenced by many elements besides his or her biology.

Biological Background Knowledge

Jeremy Strohmeyer was convicted of raping and murdering an eight-year-old girl in Nevada. He had been raised by loving, positive adoptive parents. However, an investigation revealed that his biological parents had a history of criminal behavior as well as mental illness. Would a knowledge of the boy's biological background have helped prevent his terrible crime? Or would it have condemned him to being treated with suspicion and prejudice all his life?[10]

The Family Environment

Chelsea's parents had good jobs. They always paid their bills, but only when they felt like paying them—and that was usually late. The result was that their electricity was shut off at least once a year, and every few months they got unpleasant phone calls about the mortgage payments, or the car payments, or the credit card bills. Then there was a huge fuss and an "emergency" trip to the bank or electric company or car dealer. Chelsea's parents always told her that their creditors were being unreasonable. They would get their money eventually, they said. What was the big deal?

Chelsea finished college and got a good job. When her bills arrived, she threw them on her desk and forgot about them. Only when the notices started coming in bright red ink did she pull out her checkbook and actually pay them. Chelsea was shocked when she was turned down for a car loan. She always paid her bills…eventually! What was the problem?

Parents who behave without considering the results of their behavior are actually teaching their children how to behave badly. Their children learn to think of impulsive behavior as normal at home. They naturally act impulsively when they are out of the home, sometimes with harmful results.

Children from abusive families, or children who are neglected at home, may also develop impulsive behavior as they try to cope with the poor treatment they receive. Quick action becomes the only way to survive, as these children often feel they must grab in desperation for what they need whenever they can.

This type of response can lead to serious consequences, including difficulty with relationships and even legal problems. However, some children from abusive families are so used to behaving impulsively that they continue their negative behavior when they become adults.[11]

The Immediate Environment

The situations we find ourselves in constantly inspire impulses. We are always making decisions about how to handle those impulses, and what actions to take. For example, a man had been on a diet for weeks. He successfully resisted everything fattening, especially his favorite food, ice cream. On his way home from work one afternoon he happened to drive by a brand new ice cream store. Ten minutes later, he found himself walking out with a triple scoop of fudge ripple.

But the single impulse to overeat did not ruin his diet. Later that evening, he laced up his running shoes and jogged for three miles. The next day he stayed on his diet. His loss of control was a minor slip.

However, certain situations can cause great difficulty for people suffering from impulse-control disorders. A pathological gambler who is trying to quit gambling is not likely to go to Las Vegas and be able to resist the neon lights. He will probably find himself in front of a slot machine within an hour. Similarly, a teenager who thinks that stealing will impress her friends might find herself with a lipstick in her pocket and a security guard at her elbow the next time she goes to the mall. Changing or avoiding environments may be necessary in order to control negative impulsive behaviors.

Treatment

Psychological counseling or therapy is usually helpful for people with impulse-control disorders. Cognitive and behavioral therapies show faster and more reliable results than traditional "talking" therapy for most sufferers, especially those with repeated compulsive behaviors. Cognitive therapy helps a person to identify thinking patterns that create negative emotions and reactions, and literally "rethink" them. Another cognitive technique involves carefully analyzing a situation and all the possible results of an action before acting.

Behavioral therapy makes the person aware of the problem behavior and identifies strategies to bring it under conscious control. One form of behavioral therapy, "habit reversal training," teaches a person to identify a problem action, such as pulling hair when feeling anxious, and to substitute a less harmful activity, such as clenching the fists.

Staying in a healthy, non-tempting environment is important. Finding and maintaining such an environment can require planning, including a back-up strategy in case the person ends up in a dangerous situation. A person needs to be aware if he or she is experiencing something that can make it harder to maintain control over impulses, such as a major emotional upset, feeling physically threatened, misuse of alcohol or drugs, or lack of sleep, and plan accordingly.

Complete treatment should involve members of the person's family whenever possible, since it is likely that some of them share the behaviors. Impulsive children can benefit from early intervention in the school setting to develop appropriate social skills, learn to pay attention, and lower aggression. A child's treatment is more likely to succeed when the parents are involved.[12]

Medications for Impulse-Control Disorders

Psychological treatment of ICD may be combined with psychotropic medications. These are drugs that affect the balance of chemicals in the brain. Doctors have not found a single medication that helps control negative impulsive behavior, however. There are two reasons for this. First, we have not

Types of Medications Used to Treat Impulse-Control Disorders

Tricyclic Antidepressants: Elavil, Pamelor, Tofranil, Norpramin

Selective Serotonin Re-Uptake Inhibitors: Prozac, Zoloft, Luvox, Paxil

Mood Stablilizers: lithium (used for bipolar disorder), Tegretol, Depakote (antiseizure drugs)

Antianxiety Medications: Valium, Ativan, Klonopin, Xanax

Other Antidepressants: Wellbutrin, Trazadone, Serzone.[13]

identified all of the different biological factors associated with the five impulse-control disorders. Second, we do not yet understand the complex interactions of the neurotransmitters and other chemicals in the brain.

People suffering from an ICD almost always suffer from other psychological disorders as well. In some cases, treatment for the other condition may help the impulsive behavior. This is especially true with depression and alcohol and/or substance abuse. However, the effects of the combination of disorders may mean that a particular medication does not help control the impulsive behavior, and may even make it worse.

The most commonly prescribed drug treatments for impulse-control disorders are antidepressants. Antidepressants help regulate the availability and absorption of serotonin in the system. Serotonin is the brain chemical that regulates our emotions and judgment. Medications to block the absorption of dopamine, which regulates feelings of excitement and pleasure, are also used. Other kinds of medications have been tried on an experimental basis.

3

Pyromania

Jack had been preparing for weeks. Small twigs and branches, dry grass, the freshest matches he could find. This would be his fourth fire in two months. He always chose abandoned buildings far from town. He liked to watch the roofs collapse—that was his favorite part.

He felt more and more excited as the day he had chosen drew closer. He washed and folded his special fire clothes—black pants, shirt and socks. He carefully arranged the twigs and grass in a black gym bag. His anticipation built to the point that he could not concentrate at school. He flunked a math test but he did not care. Tonight was the night.

Jack was going to set a fire, which he knew would do damage, on purpose. But Jack is not a kid who plays with matches sometimes. Jack has a disorder called pyromania. We frequently hear the term "pyromaniac" used to describe a person who has set a

People who suffer from pyromania enjoy setting fires and watching them burn.

fire. It is more accurate to call most people who set fires "arsonists" or "firesetters." The word "pyromania" describes a serious psychological disorder. A person with pyromania, like Jack, sets fires for only one reason: because he or she cannot resist the excitement of setting a fire and watching it burn.

While fire setting is unfortunately common, pyromania is rare. Studies show that less than 2 percent of all people who set fires suffer from pyromania.[1]

Pyromania occurs in adolescents and adults, but not in children. People with pyromania tend to set fires at night in a repeated pattern, rather than going on a fire-setting "binge." They prefer to work alone, and try hard not to be caught. They follow ritual fire-setting habits, and love watching fires, fire

Diagnostic Criteria
for Pyromania in the DSM-IV-TR

A. Deliberate and purposeful fire setting on more than one occasion.

B. Tension or affective arousal before the act.

C. Fascination with, interest in, curiosity about, or attraction to fire and its situational contexts (e.g., paraphernalia, uses, consequences).

D. Pleasure, gratification, or relief when setting fires, or when witnessing or participating in their aftermath.

E. The fire setting is not done for monetary gain, as an expression of sociopolitical ideology, to conceal criminal activity, to express anger or vengeance, to improve one's living circumstances, in response to a delusion or hallucination, or as a result of impaired judgment (e.g., in dementia, mental retardation, substance intoxication).

F. The fire setting is not better accounted for by Conduct Disorder, a Manic Episode, or Antisocial Personality Disorder.[2]

People with pyromania become obsessed with all aspects of fire setting, such as watching fires and fire-fighting activity.

trucks, and all fire-fighting activity. They get great emotional pleasure from setting and watching a fire.[3]

The Cost of Setting Fires

Deliberately setting a fire for any reason, including pyromania, is called arson. Arson is one of the leading causes of fires in the United States and Canada. In the United States alone, 560,000 fires a year are caused by arson. In 1998, 6,215 people were killed in fires deliberately set by children and adolescents; 30,800 were injured, and 11 billion dollars worth of damage to property was done. Of every 100 people who die in arson-caused fires, 85 are children.[4]

Profile of a Firesetter

Because of the high cost of fires in lives and dollars, police, fire investigators, and insurance companies are very interested in identifying people who start fires. Such people are called firesetters. A firesetter, sometimes also called an arsonist, is a person who has the impulse to set fires for reasons not related to the usual, socially accepted uses of fire.[5] Burning trash in rural areas, lighting a fire in a fireplace, or using a Bunsen burner in a science lab are all normal ways to use fire. A person with pyromania is considered a firesetter because setting a fire for excitement is not a normal reason to set a fire.

One method of identifying firesetters is called profiling. A profile is a set of typical characteristics of a person who does something, such as set fires. The characteristics are both physical and psychological. Profiles of firesetters suggest that most are male, Caucasian, and in their teens or early twenties. Over half of those arrested for arson are adolescents, and nearly half of these adolescents are under 15 years of age. This is the only major category of crime in which more young people than adults are involved.[6] Some are involved in other criminal activities or substance abuse. Although the great majority of firesetters are boys, more and more girls appear to be engaging in this destructive behavior.[7]

Most people who turn to fire setting have faced a variety of family, psychological, and environmental challenges. As children, their homes were often troubled, with uninvolved, absent, or mentally ill parents. They frequently had trouble in school, and might have performed poorly on standard intelligence tests. As they grew older, they may have had trouble establishing and maintaining friendships, and often felt alone. Their lack of sensitivity for the feelings of others may have led them to abuse younger children or the pets in their homes. Stressful events left them feeling unable to cope and sometimes suicidal. Fire setting became a way to act out their feelings, providing a voice for unhappiness and anger they could not find anywhere else.[8]

Despite the development of profiles for firesetters, very few are ever caught. The arrest rate for arson is only 15 percent. The conviction rate is only 3 percent.[9]

Motives for Setting Fires

Firesetters have many different reasons for lighting fires. The most common reasons are:[10]

- *Revenge.* A hardware store owner in Hong Kong was burned on over 40 percent of his body when a former employee set the store on fire. The employee was angry because he had been fired.[11] Revenge is the most common of all motives for setting fires. Women who feel rejected or abused may set a fire for revenge.

- *Insurance or other financial fraud.* This is the second most common motive. Men are more likely than women to set fires for financial gain. The professional "torch" falls into this category. He or she usually acts rationally, and does not have the psychological problems associated with other fire setters.

38

- *Concealing another crime.* Occasionally a person kills someone and sets fire to the building where the body is, trying to make the death look accidental.

- *Trying to be a hero.* Vanity firesetters may join fire companies and try to look good by setting fires and being the first on the scene.

- *Vandalism, boredom, thrillseeking, or peer group pressure.* Children and adolescents are most likely to set fires for these reasons.

- *Experimentation with fire, and the power it represents.* This motive is also more typical of children than of adults.

- *Terrorism or social protest.* Arsonists bombed a bank in Greece after a child with leukemia died. The bank had refused to release money donated for the child's medical treatment.[12]

- *"Communicative arson."* This is a cry for help from a person who feels that he or she cannot get attention any other way. Children who are in abusive living situations may set fires in order to be noticed. Once the need behind the act is addressed, the fire setting usually stops.[13]

- *Attempting to injure oneself.* This reason shows up more commonly among women than among men.

- *Severe mental illness,* such as hallucinations or delusions, may cause some people to set fires.

- *Pyromania.* This is the rarest motive of all.

Thanks, Mom?

Joy Glassman of Mount Shasta, California, was just trying to help her son out. He was a seasonal firefighter with the United States Forest Service, and received extra pay for each fire he fought. According to the California Forestry Department, Mrs. Glassman set five small fires in Shasta Trinity National Forest, because she knew that her son would be called to help put them out.

Her son knew nothing of his mother's activities. However, he decided to resign from the Forest Service. His mother faces twenty years in prison if convicted of arson.[14]

Types of Firesetters

For purposes of identification and treatment, firesetters are classified into two major types: minor and severe. A person with pyromania is considered a severe firesetter.

The Minor Firesetter

Tyler found school boring. He always knew the answer to the questions the teacher asked. He finished his homework in half the time the other kids needed. But he did not like to go home after school. His mother was usually asleep, passed out on the couch with a bottle in her hand. His dad had left long ago.

So he hung around school as long as he could after classes were over. One day, he found a pack of matches in a desk in an empty classroom. He dropped a few papers into the trash can and lit a match. Nice little fire. Safe. No one was hurt. He felt better, like he had destroyed something that was bothering him. He started lighting these little fires everyday. One day he dropped the match into the trash can without looking. A huge flame burst out, along with a strong chemical smell. Something else was in the can. The flames leaped to the bulletin board, and it caught on fire. Tyler ran out of the room, but not fast enough to avoid getting caught.

Minor fire setting is defined as accidentally or occasionally starting fires. It may be caused by curiosity, or by enjoyment of the sound, light, and warmth of the fire itself. However, Tyler's fire destroyed six classrooms at his school. Fortunately, no one was hurt. But Tyler was in big trouble. One "minor" fire was enough to send Tyler to a juvenile detention center for a long time.

The Severe Firesetter

The deliberate, planned, and persistent starting of fires is called severe fire setting. This definition includes pyromania. A person who behaves in this way intends to do harm, and feels little or no remorse after the event. Severe firesetters suffer from other, usually serious, psychological problems. They are often grappling with feelings of anger, resentment, and rage that they cannot express in a socially acceptable way. They have little control over their impulses and are fascinated with fire.[15] Severe firesetters are very likely to continue to set fires, even while in treatment facilities.

One of the most famous mental patients in literary history had a habit of firesetting.

> …the mad lady, who was as cunning as a witch, would take the keys out of her [caretaker's] pocket, let herself out of her chamber, and go roaming about the house, doing any wild

mischief that came into her head. They say she had nearly burnt her husband in his bed once: but I don't know about that. However, on this night, she set fire first to the hangings of the room next her own, and then she got down to a lower storey, and made her way to the chamber that had been the governess's—...—and she kindled the bed there.

Do you recognize Mrs. Rochester from Charlotte Bronte's novel, *Jane Eyre*? What was her motive for setting fires?

Mrs. Rochester (far right), a character from Charlotte Bronte's novel, *Jane Eyre,* is one of literature's most famous firesetters.

Young Children and Fires

Children are fascinated by fire. A child may impulsively grab matches and light them just because they are within reach, or mimic a parent lighting the logs in the fireplace. This natural imitative tendency of children can have serious consequences, however. A five-year-old boy in Ohio set a fire that killed his two-year-old sister after watching a TV cartoon show in which the characters were setting fires.[16]

Children as young as one year of age may set fires as they experiment with the limits of their own power. In New York City, the average age of children setting fires is 6.7 years.[17] Children who see fires at an early age sometimes become interested in setting them. A parent who misuses fire can serve as a model for the child's misuse.

Treatment

Treatment to decrease fire-setting behavior varies, depending on the person's age and the reason the person is setting the fires. No special treatment for pyromania has been identified.

Young children are the easiest to treat. They do not realize how destructive their behavior is, and they usually do not intend to cause real harm. Educating children about the damage fires cause, satisfying their fascination with fires and fire fighting in harmless ways, and keeping matches and lighters away from them stops fire setting in all but the most determined child. A child over the age of six who is setting fires should receive professional counseling.

Parents must also become involved by teaching children the results of setting fires. In some troubled families, this intervention does not occur. Fire setting may then become part of a pattern of destructive behavior. "Fire setting is one of the earliest signs of trouble in children," says Patricia Mieszala, R.N., the founder of Burn Concerns, Inc., a California organization that provides information on burn prevention and juvenile fire-setting behavior. Ms. Mieszala feels that fire setting at a young age is a sign of other potential problems, and requires immediate help.[18]

Adolescent and adult firesetters face legal consequences for their actions. These consequences can include monetary fines and time in jail. Arson is classified with murder, rape, kidnapping, and robbery as a serious crime. If a person appears likely to continue to set fires, he or she will be sent to jail or a secure residential facility in order to protect others from the harm a fire can cause.

Successful treatment must take into account all aspects of the firesetter's life. In adolescents and adults, fire setting usually occurs as one of a group of negative behaviors such as aggression, lying, stealing, and vandalism. A firesetter may be struggling with anger, depression, misuse of alcohol and drugs, and even hallucinations. Some are experiencing major mental illnesses such as schizophrenia (separation of thoughts and feelings). Usually, each firesetter has a whole set of different reasons for starting fires. These reasons must be identified before effective treatment can start.

Because firesetters often live in poorly functioning families, treatment should include services for the whole family whenever possible. Learning to communicate and to manage anger are two ways to improve the family environment which will make a person less likely to set fires as a way of expressing feelings.

Minor firesetters are sometimes allowed to continue living at home while they receive counseling, fire safety education, and social skills training. However, if they have caused great harm, as Tyler did, they will be treated like severe firesetters. Severe firesetters are usually placed in secure residential treatment facilities, because the possibility of their starting more fires is so high. A psychiatric hospital may be the best treatment location for a person who is severely mentally disturbed. A severe firesetter also receives counseling and behavior modification therapy along with fire safety and awareness education.

Little research has been conducted on medication for fire-setting behavior. Some studies suggest that a low level of serotonin may be associated with aggressive behavior such as fire setting. Anti-depressant medications that raise the level of serotonin in the brain might be helpful, especially when the firesetter also suffers from depression.

Fire setting is a problem that affects everyone. Prevention, intervention, and treatment must begin with the whole community. Waiting until a fire is set and a person is arrested is too late for everyone concerned.

4

Kleptomania

Fourteen-year-old Gennifer dropped a pair of earrings into her pocket and turned slowly away from the department store counter. No one had seen her. She walked out of the store, her heart pounding. Outside, she felt a rush of excitement, and a twinge of guilt. She had gotten away with shoplifting again.

When she got home, she threw the earrings into the closet. She had no intention of wearing them. They were way too ugly. They sat on a pile of other stolen, unused clothes and jewelry.

Two years after the earring incident, Gennifer was finally caught shoplifting. Fortunately, she was not arrested. But she did have to attend a long series of counseling sessions. Her father took away her brand-new driver's license and grounded her for months.[1]

The Cost of Theft

Although some people steal from friends or relatives, most theft occurs in retail establishments. Shoplifting (taking merchandise from a store without paying for it) costs storeowners in the United States anywhere from $8 billion to $50 billion a year. This number is rising: the number of shoplifting incidents rose 45 percent between 1986 and 1995, while other forms of theft declined. Two million Americans are charged with shoplifting each year. One in every eleven Americans shoplifts at least once. A third of those caught are under 18 years of age. Storeowners spend nearly a billion dollars a year trying to deter shoplifters. Stealing, because it increases prices, costs every American family $350 a year.[2]

Stealing does not cause problems for storeowners alone. Between June 2000 and April 2001, three people died from injuries they received while being apprehended for suspected shoplifting.[3]

Professional and Amateur Shoplifters

There are two kinds of shoplifters: professional and amateur.

The Professional

A small number of people support themselves as professional thieves. Professionals dress as prosperous customers and concentrate on expensive items. Usually they work in teams. Like actors, they rehearse the act of stealing, and practice sounding surprised and remorseful if they are caught. A professional thief may steal for a fence, someone who will pay the thief and then sell the illegally obtained goods for a profit.

Amateur Thieves

Amateur shoplifters are far more common than professionals. Their nervous behavior makes them easier to spot than the pros. But their sheer numbers cost businesses much more money.

One group of amateurs are the household shoppers. These thieves do their stealing during regular shopping trips to their favorite stores. When they find something they cannot afford, they simply steal it. A large purse placed in the front of the shopping cart allows them to conceal small, expensive extras as they make their other selections. These shoppers may eat things they never pay for while shopping, or switch price tickets to save a few dollars. Despite their amateur status, their behavior is planned and purposeful theft.

Impulsive Shoplifters

Impulsive shoplifters make up the largest group of amateur thieves. They steal for many reasons.

Sometimes a person steals in response to a stressful or traumatic event in his or her life. John W. Shannon, the acting Secretary of the United States Army, was caught stealing clothing from a store in Virginia. He had just found out that he had been passed over for the permanent appointment as Secretary of the Army.

Other people put things in their pockets or purses without thinking. They are shocked and ashamed when they are stopped outside the store. These absent-minded people are often preoccupied with personal problems. They are not even aware that they have taken something.

Some very depressed people steal in order to intensify their feelings of self-doubt. "Stealing is bad, I am bad, so I steal," goes their thinking.[4]

Give Me A Plate, Hold The Food

Upscale restaurants have a growing problem with customers who feel entitled to take home the glasses or silverware after a good meal. Some seem to feel that the price of the meal is so high it should include the table decorations. Others want a memento of an important event. These people would never think of their actions as stealing. Whatever the cause, restaurant owners have to decide whether to confront potential thieves and lose their business, or just mark up their prices.[5]

Young people from all economic groups engage in shoplifting. Usually they steal in order to gain acceptance by their friends, either as an initiation rite or to get something their friends have that they cannot afford. Juveniles do not usually plan their shoplifting activities, or think realistically about the consequences of getting caught.[6]

Kleptomania

Another type of impulsive stealing is kleptomania. The word is derived from the Greek words *kleptein* ("to steal") and *mania* ("madness"). Kleptomania differs from the above categories of thievery in that there is no obvious reason for the stealing. Kleptomania appears to be a rare disorder. Perhaps only 5 percent of shoplifters are kleptomaniacs. The majority are female. Although precise figures are impossible to obtain, one estimate says that of $9.7 billion lost because of shoplifting each year, $485 million is due to kleptomania.[7]

Characteristics of Kleptomania

Kleptomania begins early, usually in the teen years. However, the disorder may remain hidden for fifteen years or longer.[8]

Most people with kleptomania describe an unbearable or overwhelming tension that drives them to commit an act they know is wrong. They steal things they do not need and often do not even like. When the theft is successful they are then filled with relief, almost like a "high." During the act of stealing, they do not think about the consequences of their actions.

People who steal compulsively always have another psychological disorder. Depression or anxiety are the two most common. Many suffer from eating disorders, substance abuse, and obsessive-compulsive disorder.[9] Their home lives may be abusive, neglectful, or chaotic. Some people who suffer from kleptomania may be so overwhelmed by their inability to control their behavior that they attempt suicide.

History of Kleptomania

Stealing something one does not need has a long history. Around A.D. 400, the African bishop St. Augustine wrote in his autobiography about an incident in his youth:

Even I wanted to steal, and I did steal, although I was not driven by poverty....For I stole something that I had a lot of myself, and much better. And I did not want to enjoy that which I had stolen, but I enjoyed the act of stealing and doing wrong.

The young Augustine and his friends stole "huge loads" of pears from a neighbor's tree, ate a few, and threw the remaining fruit to the pigs.[11]

The aunt of the English novelist Jane Austen was arrested for taking a card of lace from a shop in 1799. Wealthy and socially

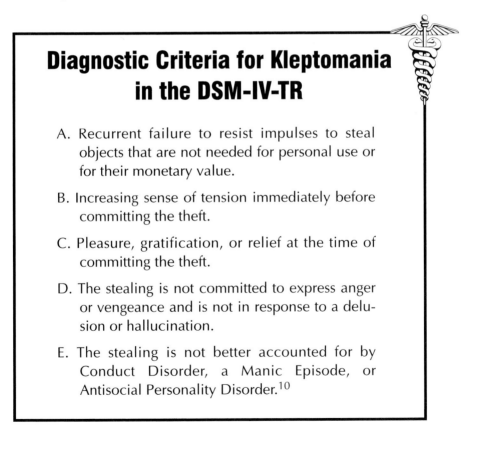

Diagnostic Criteria for Kleptomania in the DSM-IV-TR

A. Recurrent failure to resist impulses to steal objects that are not needed for personal use or for their monetary value.

B. Increasing sense of tension immediately before committing the theft.

C. Pleasure, gratification, or relief at the time of committing the theft.

D. The stealing is not committed to express anger or vengeance and is not in response to a delusion or hallucination.

E. The stealing is not better accounted for by Conduct Disorder, a Manic Episode, or Antisocial Personality Disorder.[10]

well-connected, Mrs. Jane Leigh-Perrot obviously had the means to pay for the item. At her trial, the store owner was attacked in court for daring to accuse such a respectable person. Mrs. Leigh-Perrot was acquitted.

The term *kleptomania* was coined by Drs. Étienne Esquirol and Charles Chrétien Marc in France in 1838. They defined it as "a conscious, irresistible urge to steal present in an otherwise normal individual." One hundred years later, a German psychiatrist, Fritz Wittels, described kleptomaniacs as "criminal psychopaths."[12]

The 1850s saw the appearance of a new phenomenon in Paris. Huge department stores, as large as whole city blocks, grew like mushrooms. They became wildly popular, especially among middle-class Parisian women. London, New York, Chicago, and Philadelphia quickly followed Paris' lead and built their own megastores. The French novelist Émile Zola (1840–1902) was fascinated by these stores and the women who shopped in them. He wrote a novel about one of these huge stores, called *The Ladies' Paradise*, in 1883. In the novel, the store owner proudly described three kinds of thieves that patronized his establishment, including kleptomaniacs. Kleptomania, according to the proprietor, was a new kind of mental illness that afflicted women shoppers. It was brought about by the sheer abundance of goods available in his new, wonderful superstore. He seems to have taken the appearance of kleptomaniacs as a compliment!

The diagnosis of kleptomania was invoked as a legal defense in a trial in Wyoming in 1893. Stella F. Gatlin and her husband managed the post office in Myersville, Wyoming. She was accused of stealing from registered letters. Her claim that she was unable to control her behavior because of kleptomania was rejected. Stella became the first woman jailed in Wyoming for committing a federal crime.[13] Kleptomania is still not admitted as a legal defense for a crime.

Kleptomania was included in the first *Diagnostic and Statistical Manual of Mental Disorders* in 1952, but only as a symptom in another disorder. It did not appear at all in the second edition. In 1980, kleptomania, along with all the other impulse-control disorders except for trichotillomania, made its first appearance as an independent diagnosis in the third edition. It remains an independent diagnosis in the fourth revised edition of the DSM, published in 2000.

Treatment

A person who steals compulsively does not usually come forward and confess. If they are not caught, people can steal for many years. Long-term repetition allows the stealing habit to become a part of a person's personality. It is difficult to let it go, even when the person desperately wants to stop.

Because people do not want to be known as thieves, a person receiving counseling for another problem may never tell the counselor about the stealing behavior. Many practitioners do not know to look for such hidden behavior. As a result, the stealing continues without treatment.

Psychological Treatments

Behavioral therapy focuses on the behavior and not the reasons why a person does something. In one behavioral technique, the patient is taught to pair an unpleasant feeling with the desire he is trying to control. For example, a person who feels the urge to steal might try:

53

- holding his breath until he is uncomfortable;

- pinching his wrist; or

- thinking of becoming sick.

This approach is called aversive behavioral intervention.

In cognitive therapy, a patient learns to think through a situation from start to final consequences. A person might imagine being arrested and sent to jail after stealing, or think about how her parents and friends will react to her arrest for shoplifting. This technique can be very effective for impulsive people.

Some people try to avoid going to stores. This is seldom a practical approach, because everyone needs to purchase things occasionally. It can also result in feeling isolated.

Psychotherapy is a long-term intervention designed to help the patient tap into unconscious reasons for actions. When the patient becomes aware of the reasons, so the theory goes, he or she can stop acting on them. This approach is often combined with behavioral and cognitive treatment.[14]

Medications for Kleptomania

The biochemical background of kleptomania is not well understood. Kleptomania afflicts many people who also suffer from depression and anxiety, but medications for these disorders do not always improve the stealing behavior. Sometimes, medication decreases kleptomaniac behavior for a short time, but it usually returns in full force.

One person with kleptomania who also suffered from obsessive-compulsive disorder did stop stealing while on one type of antidepressant.[15] But another found that antidepressants only helped her feel less guilty when she stole![16]

One experimental treatment involves the use of naltrexone, a drug which cuts down on the "high" that alcoholics get when they drink. The hope is that naltrexone can block the high, or the relief, that kleptomaniacs feel when they steal. Without the sensation of relief, people should be less eager to steal. A clinical trial of naltrexone is in the works.[17]

She Stole a Warehouse

One of the most successful shoplifters of all is now inmate number 288722 in the Utah State Prison. Beverly McGill looked like a model citizen. She was married to a police officer and was the mother of two teenage daughters. However, she had a secret. She had been a kleptomaniac since she was eight years old.

Beverly had over a quarter of a million dollars in pilfered merchandise in her basement when she was caught. She stole from every shopping mall in her hometown of Ogden, Utah, sometimes using her daughters to distract store personnel. Wedding gowns, shoes that did not fit, video tapes she did not watch, and china angel figurines all made it to her basement. Eventually, she had so much stuff she started selling it to her friends.

Beverly McGill was finally arrested, tried, and sentenced to fifteen years in prison. Part of the reason for her long sentence was the judge's feeling that she had caused grave harm to her daughters by involving them in her thievery. Beverly receives no treatment for kleptomania in jail. Her husband, who knew what she was doing but who could not bring himself to turn her in, spent six months in jail and lost his job.[18]

Shop 'Til You Drop

Another compulsive consumption disorder appears to be related to kleptomania. Some people bring home as many items from a store as Beverly did. However, they have paid for their purchases. Like Beverly, they do not need the things that crowd their shelves and closets. But they cannot stop buying them. These people do not suffer from kleptomania. They are compulsive shoppers.

Compulsive shopping does not usually result in jail time. However, it can bring serious financial problems to the shopper and her or his family. This disorder afflicts people of all income levels. One estimate claims that between 2 and 8 percent of Americans have spending problems that can be classified as compulsive.[19] Like kleptomaniacs, most compulsive shoppers are women.

Compulsive shoppers say they experience the tension and relief cycle common to kleptomania and other impulse control disorders. However, there is an important difference between kleptomania and compulsive shopping in the types of items the person selects. A kleptomaniac takes things of no obvious personal value to her or him. Compulsive shoppers purchase items that have emotional meaning for them. Usually they are expensive, tasteful items whose purchase makes the buyers feel important. For example, men typically buy stereo equipment or furniture. Women concentrate on upscale clothing, jewelry, and cosmetics. Purchasing these types of goods gives the shoppers a much-needed, if temporary, boost to their self image. Studies have shown that self-esteem among compulsive shoppers is extremely low.[20]

5

Pathological Gambling

Cory loved Fridays. That was the day his mom brought home instant lottery tickets. Fridays felt like Christmas to the eight-year-old boy. He loved the idea that each shiny ticket held the promise of a fortune in winnings.

At age ten, Cory was playing penny poker with his friends as often as he could. Winning made him feel important. However, he did not always win. One day he lost $150. He had to steal $100 from his father to cover his debt.

As a teenager, Cory started betting on horse races and basketball and football games. He became a bookie, running bets for his friends from the high school parking lot. He was stealing from stores to finance his gambling losses. Finally, he got caught shoplifting. Only then did he find treatment to control his serious pathological gambling.[1]

Pathological gamblers sometimes resort to stealing money to cover their debts.

Pathological Gambling

Lots of people play the slots at a casino once a year, buy lottery tickets, or play penny poker every so often with their friends. This is called social gambling: gambling with friends for a limited amount of time, knowing what you can afford to lose and stopping there. But some people find that gambling is more than a social pastime. A weekly stop at the convenience store to buy lottery tickets turns into a daily trip. The occasional visit to the casinos becomes frequent. The amount of money lost becomes

Diagnostic Criteria for Pathological Gambling in the DSM-IV

A. Persistent and recurrent maladaptive gambling behavior as indicated by five (or more) of the following:

1. is preoccupied with gambling (e.g., preoccupied with reliving past gambling experiences, handicapping or planning the next venture, or thinking of ways to get money with which to gamble)

2. needs to gamble with increasing amounts of money in order to achieve the desired excitement

3. has repeated unsuccessful efforts to control, cut back, or stop gambling

4. is restless or irritable when attempting to cut down or stop gambling

5. gambles as a way of escaping from problems or of relieving a dysphoric mood (e.g., feelings of helplessness, guilt, anxiety, depression)

6. after losing money gambling, often returns another day to get even ("chasing" one's losses)

7. lies to family members, therapist, or others to conceal the extent of involvement with gambling

8. has committed illegal acts such as forgery, fraud, theft, or embezzlement to finance gambling

9. has jeopardized or lost a significant relationship, job, or educational or career opportunity because of gambling

10. relies on others to provide money to relieve a desperate financial situation caused by gambling

B. The gambling behavior is not better accounted for by a Manic Episode.

significant. The person borrows, lies, or even steals to cover up the losses.

What is the difference? It is not the kind of game the person plays. It is not the environment, whether casino, downtown bar, or convenience store. What makes a difference is the attitude of the gambler. When the gambler cannot stop until the last dollar is gone, and finds the impulse to gamble becoming stronger as the gambling continues, he or she is suffering from pathological, or compulsive, gambling. This kind of unstoppable gambling ruins the lives of the gambler and the gambler's family. It can even cost the gambler her or his job.[2]

Characteristics of Pathological Gamblers

Pathological gamblers tend to be extroverted and constantly seek new, thrilling sensations.[3] Inside, however, they often feel alone. They frequently suffer from substance abuse, depression, and anxiety.[4] They may fall into other impulsive behaviors such as compulsive buying, repeated inappropriate sexual activity, or explosive temper tantrums.[5] Psychiatrist Dr. Loreen Rugle founded a treatment center for compulsive gamblers in Indianapolis called the Custer Center. Dr. Rugle feels that one third of compulsive gamblers may also have attention-deficit/hyperactivity disorder.[6]

Gambling can persist for twenty or thirty years before the gambler gets treatment. As the habit deepens, gamblers find they must bet more and more money in order to feel the thrill of the activity. This causes financial problems for the gambler and his or her family. Unfortunately, the gambler is so wrapped up in wagering that the needs of the family are neglected. Divorce among gamblers is common. Gamblers run a higher risk of suicide than any other group of people with impulse-control disorders.[7]

Like other forms of impulsive behavior, gambling tends to lessen as a person gets older. However, gamblers always behave more impulsively than the general population.[8]

Prevalence

The number of people who gamble has been estimated to range from 68 to 85 percent of the general population of the United States. Between 1 and 3 percent of adult gamblers fall into the pathological gambling category. Men with gambling problems outnumber women two to one. The National Gambling Impact Study Commission reported that problem gambling among young people exceeds that of adults.[9] Countries around the world are struggling with increases in gambling activity and addiction.[10]

Social scientists agree that increasing opportunities for gambling mean that greater numbers of people who have the potential for gambling addiction will develop gambling problems. Some signs of a person at risk for pathological gambling include:

- spending more money than the person planned;
- playing longer than the person planned; and
- hiding the gambling from family and friends.

When Canadian gambling laws changed, the town of Hull, in the province of Quebec, opened a casino. After the casino had operated for three years, a study found that the proportion of local residents who gambled had shot up from 13.8 percent to 60.4 percent. The proportion of people at risk for developing a gambling problem rose from 3.3 percent to 7.8 percent. The same study compared the gambling habits of a neighboring town that had no casino. That town actually experienced a decrease in the number of people gambling and in those with serious gambling problems.[11]

Gambling Begins Early

Most problem gamblers recall that their betting behavior began early in their lives. Children as young as eight may be gambling regularly.[12]

Eighty-five percent of teens gamble at least once. Some teens gamble in order to get money they need, but most are trying to get lucky, believing they can beat the odds and be a hero, or get rich quickly. Teenagers can be very susceptible to the lure of gambling: 15 percent of teens experience personal or financial problems from gambling, and 5.7 percent of adolescents fall into the serious, pathological gambler category.[13] These students frequently skip school and neglect homework in order to gamble.

Teenagers can be susceptible to gambling because they may see it as a quick way to get rich.

They may turn to stealing, as Cory did, in order to finance their gaming habits.

Experimenting with games of chance is a normal way for children and adolescents to learn about taking chances and evaluating risks. However, this innocent pastime can get out of hand if other factors intervene. A stressful event, such as the death of a parent or problems at school, may be the first impetus to gamble. In this case, gambling provides an escape from unhappiness. It may also seem glamorous to a person unhappy with his or her life.

Gambling is an Ancient Pastime

Ancient societies in Egypt, Japan, and Persia have left records documenting the popularity of gambling. A famous epic from ancient India, the *Mahabharata*, tells the story of a king who lost his kingdom because he was addicted to gambling. One of the king's enemies, a skillful cheat, knew that the king could not say no when the dice were rolled. He challenged the king to a game. As they played, the king lost larger and larger amounts of gold and jewels to his dishonest opponent. Then, the king wagered his palace, lands, and remaining possessions.

After losing all his material goods, he bet each of his relatives, finally betting and losing himself. Amazingly, his adversary returned all of his lost possessions, and restored the king's own freedom. Shortly thereafter, the man challenged the king to another game. Sure enough, he lost all his possessions and his own freedom again. This time, he did not get them back.

Gambling ran wild in the prosperous English towns of the eighteenth century. Anything was considered suitable material for a bet. People ate live cats in order to win small sums. The oddsmakers gave four to one against King George II being killed in battle in 1743. Wagering on sports of all kinds was common and extravagant. By the time he had reached the age of twenty-five, Charles James Fox (1749–1806), a close friend of the future King George IV, had lost £140,000 at gaming, an amount worth millions of dollars today.[14]

The original thirteen United States drew on lotteries for a large portion of their funds in the early days, as did many of the newly-founded Ivy League universities. George Washington and Thomas Jefferson promoted lotteries as a way to raise public funds. Bribery scandals and misuse of money raised in this way led to the abolition of lotteries and most forms of gambling by 1900. The public maintained a negative view of gambling until 1964, when New Hampshire reintroduced a state lottery. It was an instant and rousing success.

Gambling is Everywhere Today

Now, all but two states allow some form of legalized gambling, whether it is lotteries, casinos, or wagering on horse and dog races. State lotteries brought in $16.5 billion in 1997.[15]

Gambling and games of chance are hard to avoid. Football pools blossom in offices around the country every fall. Churches sponsor trips to casinos. States advertise their lotteries as helping senior citizens. A car dealer offers a chance to win a new car just for taking a test drive.

The Pros

A small number of people make their living by gambling in casinos. Professional gamblers are not pathological gamblers. They are highly disciplined and follow a strict system to beat the house odds. They stop as soon as their losses begin. Casinos

Las Vegas, Nevada, is famous for its casinos and gambling. Nevada and Oregon are the only places in the United States where it is legal to bet on sports.

watch for professional gamesters and throw them out as soon as they see them at work.

Patriotic Gambling?

Even the military sponsors gambling activities. 8,000 slot and video poker machines have been provided to military personnel and their families on overseas bases. In 1999, members of the armed forces and their dependents spent $1.2 billion in these machines. It is true that over 90 percent of this amount was returned to the players in the form of winnings. However, a number of enlisted men and women have found the machines addictive. Several have been court-martialed for writing thousands of dollars in bad checks to cover their on-base gambling losses.[16]

Sports Wagering

Betting on sports events was outlawed in 1992 in all states except Nevada and Oregon. Betting on sports threatens the integrity of everyone involved in the games, at every level. However, it remains the most widespread and popular form of gambling in the United States, even on an underground level. Newspapers publish betting odds on sports events, despite the fact that such wagering is against the law. Estimates of the amounts illegally wagered on sporting events range from $80 billion to $380 billion a year.

Internet Gambling

Internet gambling is a new and rapidly growing form of betting. In the privacy of your own home, twenty-four hours a day, you can play blackjack or poker, bet on a sporting event, or play a lottery. All you need is a credit card. Profits from Internet betting grew from $445.4 million to $919.1 million in just one year, in 1997. Adolescents and young people are the biggest users of the Internet, and are the most vulnerable to this form of gambling.[17]

Biological Causes of Pathological Gambling

Three neurochemical systems appear to be involved in compulsive gambling behavior. However, little is known about their specific effect on this disorder.

Serotonin, the brain chemical associated with emotions and feelings, plays a role in controlling the impulse to begin an activity and also to stop. Studies of serotonin absorption in the brain cells of pathological gamblers have shown both abnormally high and low levels of the neurotransmitter.

Norepinephrine, the neurochemical involved in stimulating emotions and moods, is associated with risk taking. An elevated level of norepinephrine in the brain was found in one study of compulsive gamblers.

The neurochemical dopamine is linked to a person's perception of positive and negative rewards. Compulsive gamblers show abnormal levels of dopamine in the brain, which may result in their overestimating the rewards of gambling, and underestimating the consequences.[18]

Treatment

Research reveals that problem gamblers are not all alike. Some may be able to stop gambling on their own, without any treatment program. Others, however, require a lot of help in order to break their destructive habit. Many people do not seek help because they are ashamed of their behavior. Different treatments have proved to be helpful in decreasing pathological gambling.

Behavioral strategies

- Staying away from gambling environments.

- Starting new hobbies or activities to take the place of gambling.

Cognitive changes

- Remembering past problems associated with gambling.

- Thinking through ways to handle future temptations to gamble.[19]

Gamblers Anonymous (GA) is a self-help, twelve-step program modeled on the Alcoholics Anonymous program. It focuses on helping people change their problem behavior, and does not use any particular therapeutic or psychological approach. The program asks a participant to give up gambling completely, attend regular meetings, establish a friend or sponsor to call in times of temptation, and work on personal and spiritual growth. Complete confidentiality at meetings is assured. This allows the problem gambler to talk openly about his or her problems without shame or fear.[20] Gam-Anon is an organization that provides fellowship and understanding for family and friends of gamblers.

Schools are developing educational programs about the hazards of gambling. Elizabeth George, director of the North American Training Institute of Duluth, Minnesota, has created a curriculum program for grades three to eight called "Wanna Bet?" This program teaches children about the likelihood of winning games of chance, and shows them how gambling can affect all members of their families.[21]

Because gambling has such an impact on the whole family, family counseling can help all members of a gambler's family. If a person is gambling as a way to escape stress in the family, counseling can provide help for the family problems as well. Less family stress may mean less gambling.

No large-scale studies have been conducted on medications for compulsive gambling. However, some people have found that they gamble less when they take antidepressants or mood stabilizers. A gambler with another psychiatric disorder, such as depression, may notice a decrease in gambling behavior when he or she receives treatment to help the other disorder. Research in this area is urgently needed.

6

Intermittent Explosive Disorder

Two travelers approached a crossroad. Neither would yield the right of way to the other. At last one pushed past, only to be struck from behind by the other. Furious, the first man rushed back and killed the passengers in the other vehicle. Then he continued on his way, not bothering to tell anyone about the dead bodies lying on the road.

This sounds like an instance of road rage, the modern epidemic of sudden violence exploding in parking lots and on crowded freeways across the country and around the world. In fact, the story dates from around 430 B.C. The killer is King Oedipus, and one of the victims is his own father.

Children can act violently as well, and with deadly results. An eight-year-old boy in New York City was charged with criminally negligent homicide after he stabbed a four-year-old neighbor in the hallway of the apartment building their families shared. The eight-year-old and his nine-year-old brother had bullied the neighbor boy and his sister for over a year. They had teased the littler children, pushing them around and spitting on them. No one knows why the bullying turned into murder. The boy is one of the youngest people in the United States to be charged in a slaying.[1]

What is Anger?

Anger can be defined as being displeased with an event or situation. It is a basic emotion, common to all humans and animals as well.

Anger plays an important role in survival because it arouses the "fight or flight" response in our bodies. This system provides the physical and emotional stimulation for us to react quickly to a situation that could harm us. When we are angry, our hearts start pumping harder. Our stomachs stop digesting food. We breathe heavily, taking in more oxygen. Blood rushes to the muscles, preparing them to move quickly. Our senses become intently focused. Every part of our bodies concentrates on the threatening situation and gets us ready to defend ourselves.

Anger has given people the energy to make great changes in society. Anger at the system of slavery in the United States propelled Frederick Douglass (1817–1895) and Harriet Tubman (1820?–1913) to fight against oppressive laws and help win freedom for all slaves.[2]

Anger Is A Health Issue

After a surge of anger, we feel tired and drained. Our energy levels are low. The cycle of arousal and exhaustion from constant feelings of anger is associated with a host of health problems. A fast heart rate and high blood pressure increase the likelihood of heart attacks and strokes. High blood pressure can cause kidney problems as well. Headaches, stomachaches, and irritable bowel syndrome are other results of constant angry feelings. Angry people experience more colds and other illnesses because their bodies are too tired to fight off germs.

Angry people also have trouble in social situations. Work and personal relationships suffer when a person is constantly hostile.

Anger, Rage, and Violence

Anger arises when someone does something to us that we do not like, or something happens that bothers us. We can also be alone and get angry just thinking about such incidents.

Common motivations for angry feelings include:

- protection of self or family;

- revenge;

- desire for social or material status; and

- impulsive feelings.[3]

When a person feels extreme anger, it is called rage. Even rage is not harmful in and of itself. Anger and rage result in violence only when a person does not find an acceptable outlet for the angry feelings, such as talking, but instead employs physical means, such as hitting.

The law becomes involved when anger is expressed in violent actions. Rage can become a danger both to the angry person and to the rest of society. A person committing a violent act will be arrested and put into jail to halt further damage. The injured person can sue the offender for monetary damages. Restraining orders are issued to prevent the offender from going near the victim.

But do these measures work? Restraining orders can be ignored. Money cannot make up for loss of life or permanent physical injury. Jails are full of violent criminals who continue to act violently after they have been punished and released. A study of prisoners in Florida from 1993 to 1995 showed that 35.8 percent of inmates convicted of violent crimes committed another crime after they were released, compared with 26.8 percent of those whose crimes were nonviolent.[4]

Rage in Our Society

Television and newspapers report rage incidents almost every day. Anger incidents on the highways, commonly called "road rage," resulted in 218 deaths and 12,610 injuries from 1992 to 1997.[5] A particularly bizarre incident occurred near the San Jose, California, airport, on February 11, 2000. Sara McBurnett was on her way to the airport to pick up her husband when a car cut in front of her. She was unable to avoid bumping the back of the other car. She was shocked when the driver of the car jumped out and stormed back to her car. Her shock turned to horror when the man reached inside her open window, grabbed the little dog sitting on her lap, and hurled it into the oncoming traffic. The dog was run over and killed.

Police spent fourteen months hunting the suspect. Finally, a determined detective found him.[6] The man, who had a history of destructive temper tantrums, was sentenced to three years in prison, the maximum term.[7]

Another kind of travel rage occurs on airplanes. Bangor International Airport in Maine hosted two unexpected landings in one day. On one flight, a man slapped his girlfriend and she struck back. On the other, three men attacked crew members. In both cases, the belligerent passengers would not calm down, and the long-distance flights were forced to land to eject the offenders. The people involved were arrested and held in jail.[8] Statistics show that incidents of air rage around the world increased from 1,132 in 1994 to 5,416 in 1997.[9]

What is causing this increase in violent expression of anger? Some psychologists feel that our role models are violent. Many

It is not just men who sometimes inappropriately act out their angry emotions. Naomi Campbell was accused of assaulting her personal assistant, and took up boxing as a way of getting her anger out in a more constructive way.

movies and video games feature violent characters and episodes. Famous people fly off the handle and just seem to get more publicity. Boxer Mike Tyson, basketball coach Bobby Knight, and rappers Sean "Puff Daddy" Combs and Eminem are just a few celebrities whose violent behavior has won them both public notice and court appearances. And it is not just men who act out their angry emotions. Supermodel Naomi Campbell took up boxing as an outlet for anger after admitting in a Canadian court that she assaulted her personal assistant.[10] Actress Shannen Doherty was ordered to take an anger management class by a judge after she threw a beer bottle at a car.[11] If celebrities are seen acting violently, many people feel that they can, too.

Others suggest that a sense of entitlement, meaning, "I deserve special treatment just because I am me," is increasing in our society. A person who feels this way takes losing a convenient parking space at the mall as a personal insult. Waiting half an hour for a drink on an airplane results in a temper tantrum. An "entitled" person feels justified in attacking anyone who gets in the way.

Poor parenting and poor parental role modeling are blamed by many. Children see their parents exploding into violence over an umpire's call at a kid's baseball game, and they proceed to act the same way.

Whatever the causes, violent expressions of rage are serious, and are increasing.

Anger At Work

One million workers are assaulted in the workplace each year in the United States. Violent incidents at work cost businesses more than $36 billion in 1995.[12] The problem is not confined to this country. One quarter of British workers interviewed in one study had experienced "a stand-up row with a fellow worker," the British term for an incident of desk rage.[13]

One large company in the U.S. is taking steps to combat this growing problem. The accounting firm of Ernst and Young has built a training and communication center in Indianapolis that features tanks of peacefully swimming fish, an indoor putting green, and a relaxation room with recliners and quiet music. The

Diagnostic Criteria for Intermittent Explosive Disorder in the DSM-IV-TR

A. Several discrete episodes of failure to resist aggressive impulses that result in serious assaultive acts or destruction of property.

B. The degree of aggressiveness expressed during the episodes is grossly out of proportion to any precipitating psychosocial stressors.

C. The aggressive episodes are not better accounted for by another mental disorder (e.g., Antisocial Personality Disorder, Borderline Personality Disorder, a Psychotic Disorder, a Manic Episode, Conduct Disorder, or Attention-Deficit/Hyperactivity Disorder) and are not due to the direct physiological effects of a substance (e.g., a drug of abuse, a medication) or a general medical condition (e.g., head trauma, Alzheimer's disease).[14]

motivation for these perks? The desire to combat stress on the job that might lead to violence.[15]

Impulsive Anger

Only recently has there been an awareness that some people become extremely angry for little or no reason. People who in the past were described as "having a short fuse" might now be diagnosed as having Intermittent Explosive Disorder (IED). IED was not included in the Diagnostic and Statistical Manual until 1980.

Prevalence

It is difficult to calculate the number of people with intermittent explosive disorder. Very few people are willing to admit having problems managing their temper. Even fewer wish to acknowledge an anger disorder. One estimate suggests that at least 20 percent of adults have anger levels high enough to constitute a health hazard.[16] Whatever the numbers, however, IED is definitely on the rise.

Most of those diagnosed with IED are men. Intermittent explosive disorder usually begins between late adolescence and age thirty, although young children sometimes exhibit unpredictable violent behavior.[17] Age does not appear to lessen the severity of IED. A one-hundred-year-old Miami man was arrested for pouring gasoline over his thirty-eight-year-old girlfriend. He claimed that she was flirting with other men. Two years earlier, at age ninety-eight, Hermenergildo Rojas had spent three days in jail after a violent argument with a bus driver.[18]

Childish Rage

Four-year-old Derrick Robie was killed by thirteen-year-old Eric Smith, who suffers from intermittent explosive disorder.

Thirteen-year-old Eric Smith was tried and convicted as an adult for the murder of four-year-old Derrick Robie. Eric could give no explanation for why he killed the little boy, who was walking to a nearby park to play kickball. A psychiatrist testified at his trial that Eric suffers from IED and feels that, without treatment, he may kill again.

Eric received a sentence of nine years to life. He will stay in a juvenile facility until he turns eighteen, at which time he will join the adult prison population.[19]

Features of Intermittent Explosive Disorder

An important difference between intermittent rage disorder and other expressions of anger is the lack of an obvious cause for the IED outburst. We can understand a person who blows up because a child has been injured by a drunk driver, even though we do not condone a violent reaction. However, a series of seemingly unmotivated outbursts is difficult to understand.

The anger outbursts of IED are usually not constant. They run in cycles, or episodes. This makes an outburst difficult to predict.[20] During a cycle, a person may experience two or more outbursts a week.

People experiencing rage attacks do not always feel the rising tension before acting and the relief after the act that are common to the other impulse-control disorders. They do report feeling impulsive urges before acting. Many people feel very guilty after they act, but some experience relief and even pleasure.

Almost all people with intermittent explosive disorder suffer from a mood disorder such as depression. Many also experience anxiety and other impulse-control disorders. A large number have migraine headaches.[21]

People with intermittent explosive disorder frequently suffer from one of two other syndromes: bipolar disorder and substance abuse.

Bipolar Disorder

In bipolar disorder, also called manic-depression, a person's moods swing from deep depression to great excitement. When depressed, the person feels no energy or interest in anything. He or she may have a very negative self-image and even consider suicide. When the mood swings to manic, the person is suddenly full of energy. He or she can go without food or sleep, and take on hundreds of new projects. These projects are abandoned when the depressive swing recurs.

The moods may alternate over a period of weeks or months. Some people have more depressed or more manic episodes. A few people experience a rapid cycling of moods, swinging from one to the other several times a day.

A Girl With Bipolar Disorder

Twelve-year-old Sarah was depressed for six months. She did little schoolwork, dropped all her friends, and never touched the piano she had loved to play. Her parents were thrilled when they heard the sound of the piano keys one afternoon. They were also delighted to see her finish her homework without being nagged.

However, they were less happy to hear the piano again in the middle of the night. Sarah could not go to sleep. She giggled constantly, and kept waking her parents up to talk to them. The next day at school, she got into trouble for disrupting her class with her constant laughing and clowning. She was sent home from school.

This disruptive behavior and sleeplessness lasted for two weeks. At that time, Sarah lapsed back into her depression.[22]

Substance Abuse

Misuse of drugs and alcohol complicates any situation. In the case of intermittent explosive disorder, these substances decrease a person's control over his or her emotions, and make a violent outburst more likely. Studies of explosive people show that almost all of them misuse alcohol or drugs.

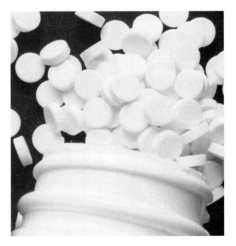

Drug or alcohol abuse can contribute to violent outbursts in people who suffer from intermittent explosive disorder.

Biology of Intermittent Explosive Disorder

The impulse of anger, like all strong emotions, originates in the limbic system of the brain. Normally, the frontal lobes of the cortex (the higher centers of the brain) intercept the impulse from the limbic system and help the person calm down. In the brain of a person with IED, however, the cortex does not exert enough control over the angry feeling. The limbic system takes over, and the anger explodes into a rage incident.

Researchers have found evidence of decreased levels of activity in the frontal lobes of the brains of violent criminals. The lower-than-normal levels of activity may explain why these people do not resist the impulses to do harm.

Low levels of serotonin, which is involved in the expression and control of impulses, have also been found in many studies of violent criminals.

Other research has identified problems with language and communication in people with anger problems. Language allows us to understand our feelings and put them into perspective. Language also lets us delay acting out on an impulse. A person who experiences difficulty using language, and who feels frustrated communicating with other people, may be at risk to develop IED.[23]

Treatment

Three kinds of psychological therapy are commonly employed to help people understand and manage explosive behavior.

1. *Behavioral therapy*: Behavioral therapy seeks to change the behavior by teaching a person to substitute less harmful forms of behavior for violent outbursts.

2. *Cognitive therapy*: Cognitive therapies help people imagine being in an anger-provoking situation and reacting calmly.

3. *Social skills training*: Social skills training can improve the way a person interacts with other people.[24]

In the case of a child who behaves violently, the whole community, including family and school, must become involved. Children need role models who express anger in non-violent ways. They also need home and school environments that encourage honest self-expression and discourage bullying. They must learn to avoid excessive alcohol and illegal drugs. Easy access to weapons, which allows a temper tantrum to turn tragic, must be prevented.

When domestic violence between husband and wife is involved, the partner being injured must feel he or she can talk about the abuse without experiencing more harm. Both partners must be committed to staying together, and to stopping the violence. Both may need counseling.

There are no drugs that work specifically on IED, but medications for other psychological problems may be helpful in controlling anger outbursts. Some have found improvement using drugs for bipolar disorder symptoms. Others have found that antidepressant medications lessened their angry outbursts.

How To Control Anger

Feeling angry does not necessarily mean becoming violent. There are several ways to handle angry feelings.

Remove yourself from the situation causing your emotional response, if possible. Counting to ten can be part of this strategy.

Breathing deeply, squeezing and releasing your fists, or shaking your arms and legs might help you relax.

Recognize that anger is often caused by fear. Figure out what you are afraid of.[25] Ideally, you should then be able to express your feelings in a way that gets your point across while respecting the feelings and rights of others. In this way, you will be able to do something about the cause of your anger.

Sometimes, however, this is not possible. When this is the situation, keeping your feelings to yourself can be healthy, as long as you do not ignore them. For example, Amanda was surprised to feel angry when she learned that her grandmother was dying. Obviously, she could not tell her grandmother how she felt. After she discovered that it is common to feel angry and rejected when a loved one is dying, she spent some time wrestling with her emotions. Amanda decided that she would take care of her grandmother's beloved roses for her as a way to channel her anger and grief. Amanda was able to convert her negative emotions into a constructive activity.

Another way to handle angry feelings is to acknowledge them and focus on calming yourself down, rather than expressing them or acting on them. This approach is appropriate when you know what is making you angry but you cannot do anything about it. This is a good strategy to use when you are stuck in a traffic jam.

Dr. Peter Panzarino, chair of the department of psychiatry at Cedars Sinai Medical Center in Los Angeles, feels that the best way to deal with rage is to prevent it from occurring in the first place. He suggests the following strategies:

- Allow plenty of time to get places and to complete projects.

- Set achievable goals and do not try to do too much at one time.

- Have friends who support you.

- Do not keep going when you are tired.

- Watch for the physical signs of anger: headache, perspiration, muscle tension, edginess.

- Avoid alcohol and drugs.[26]

Bottling up anger, rather than expressing or redirecting it, can lead to other problems. Gossiping about people behind their backs or attacking people indirectly are signs of hidden anger. Constant negative remarks may be masking anger as well.

Anger Management

Thousands of people convicted of violent crimes are being sent to anger management classes instead of to jail. These classes are designed to help people who express rage impulsively, and not those who commit premeditated violent acts. The focus of these classes is on developing understanding for others' points of view, methods of self-control, problem solving, and appropriate ways to communicate.

These programs usually run for about eight weeks. Most psychologists feel that this is too short a time to change angry behavior. In order to change habitual angry responses, at least one year is necessary. Some programs have added follow-up components to address this need.[27]

7

Trichotillomania

Carolyn Humphrey just could not get ready for work on time. The problem was her hair. It always felt itchy, so she would pull out individual strands and examine them carefully. Then she would wash and rewash her hair. The whole process took up to three hours every morning. Her employer was understanding about her coming in late—for a while. When she asked to work from home, however, she was fired.[1]

An irresistible urge to pull out your hair is called trichotillomania. This term comes from the Greek words for hair *(tricho)*, pulling *(tillo)*, and frenzy *(mania)*. People with trichotillomania may yank out so much hair that they will have bald spots on their heads, or have no eyelashes or eyebrows. This behavior can drastically alter a person's appearance and cause great embarrassment. Hair pullers may avoid social situations like shopping with friends or swimming, which might force them to reveal their lack

People who suffer from trichotillomania will often avoid social situations, such as swimming.

of hair. They avoid doctors and never go to hair salons. If they also swallow the hair they pull, they can make themselves sick.

Occasional hair pulling as a response to worry or stress is not unusual. Ten to twenty percent of people do this occasionally. They do not pull enough hair to create a noticeable loss.[2]

What Exactly is Trichotillomania?

People who pull their hair usually begin by touching or stroking it. They pull one hair out at a time, and either hold the hair between the thumb and index finger or wrap it around the index finger. People tend to use their dominant hand, meaning the

85

Diagnostic Criteria for Trichotillomania in the DSM-IV-TR

A. Recurrent pulling out of one's hair resulting in noticeable hair loss.

B. An increasing sense of tension immediately before pulling out the hair or when attempting to resist the behavior.

C. Pleasure, gratification, or relief when pulling out the hair.

D. The disturbance is not better accounted for by another mental disorder and is not due to a general medical condition (e.g., a dermatological condition).

E. The disturbance causes clinically significant distress or impairment in social, occupational, or other important areas of functioning.[3]

hand they use for writing, to pull. Most people do not feel any pain when the hair comes out. The fingers used to pull the hair can develop cuts or calluses. A few people rub their hair away or pull it out with a brush.

Any body hair can be the target of trichotillomania. Most of the time people pull from the front, top and sides, or rarely the back, of the scalp. Eyelashes, eyebrows, and pubic hair may also be pulled. Occasionally a person pulls out arm or leg hair. Most people pull hair from more than one spot on their bodies. They may prefer hair that is curly or coarsely textured.

Hair pulling can occupy a great deal of a person's time. People usually pull their hair at night, and when they are alone. Many spend over an hour pulling more than 100 hairs each day. Most people examine or play with the hair that has been removed, and may save it.

A small number of people pull someone else's hair out, usually that of a child or spouse.

Prevalence

People who pull their hair out are usually so ashamed of their behavior that they do not seek treatment, despite their desperate wish to stop. Even when seeking help for other psychological problems, they may not mention pulling their hair. Surveys suggest that 2.5 percent of the general population suffers from trichotillomania. In childhood, about the same number of boys and girls exhibit hair-pulling behavior. In adulthood, the numbers of men and women who pull enough hair out to cause emotional distress remain equal. However, many more women than men seek treatment for hair pulling. Between 70 and 93 percent of patients being treated for hair pulling are female.[4] Men may try to disguise their behavior by claiming that their hair loss is due to male pattern baldness.

History

The Bible and other ancient texts describe people pulling out their hair as a response to astonishment or stress. Today, we often hear people say they are pulling their hair out when they feel frustrated, although they do not mean it in the literal sense.

The importance of hair pulling in evaluating a patient's medical condition was known to the ancient Greek doctor Hippocrates. In describing the symptoms of a woman who was severely depressed, he noted that she was scratching at and pulling out her hair

A French doctor, H. Hallopeau, coined the word trichotillomania in 1889, when he described a young man who pulled out all his body hair. Dr. Hallopeau felt that this "insanity" was long-lasting and difficult, if not impossible, to cure.[5]

In 1913, Dr. Haldin Davis was called to a British orphanage to treat 174 children who were losing their hair. When the doctor examined the children, all girls under the age of 14, he found that the hair did not seem to be pulled out, but broken off. The children were treated with daily hair washing and iodine applied to the places where the hair was broken. The hair loss stopped, only to recur a year later. The same treatment was given, and the hair breaking stopped permanently.

The doctor was not able to identify the cause of the children's behavior, but suggested it was due to some kind of infection. He did note that this and similar incidences of hair pulling or breaking in orphanages seemed to affect only young girls.[6]

Little research has been done on this mysterious disorder. Trichotillomania was included in the *Diagnostic and Statistical Manual of Mental Disorders* for the first time in the revision of the third edition, in 1987.

Why Do People Pull Their Hair Out?

About three-fourths of patients seeking help for hair pulling behavior say that they pull their hair when they feel anxious or tense. The tension may not be caused by a specific experience.

More often it is a general sensation of nervousness or worry. The people in this group say they are not consciously aware of what they are doing when they are pulling. They may be concentrating on another task, such as reading, or just relaxing. Some say they feel like they are in a trance. This is called the "automatic" style of hair pulling.

Sometimes, just being in a quiet, restful situation may encourage people to pull their hair, even if they are not experiencing any negative feelings. These situations are typically reading, watching television, getting ready for bed, being alone in the evening, and relaxing.

The remaining one-fourth of hair pullers do not pull their hair in response to stress. They find that hair pulling gives them energy. Some say it provides a release from boredom, anger, or sadness. This style of hair pulling is called "focused."[7]

People cope with anxiety, nervousness, or boredom in many different ways. Most people have two or three of the following nervous habits:

- nail or cuticle biting;
- thumb or finger sucking;
- grinding the teeth;
- knuckle cracking or biting;
- face, nose, or scab picking;
- lip, tongue, or cheek chewing or biting;
- teeth clenching;
- head banging; or
- picking at clothes.[8]

Backstreet Boy A. J. McLean picks at his right thumb when he is worried. His thumb might get gory, but he does not stop. Everyone in his family has the same habit, he says.[9]

Other Psychological Disorders Found With Trichotillomania

Trichotillomania sufferers commonly experience depression and anxiety as well. They may abuse alcohol and drugs, possibly in an attempt to self-medicate for their painful feelings. A substantial number of people with trichotillomania also have obsessive-compulsive disorder.

A. J. McLean of the singing group The Backstreet Boys picks at his thumb when he is worried about something.

Body Dysmorphic Disorder or Trichotillomania?

Body Dysmorphic Disorder (BDD) is the preoccupation with a defect in a person's appearance, real or imagined. A woman may think her nose is too big, for example, and spend hours trying to change her appearance with makeup. She may have repeated plastic surgeries, but still feel that nothing helps.

Many people with BDD also suffer from trichotillomania. However, the two disorders are not the same. A person with BDD pulls hair in order to improve her or his appearance. A person with trichotillomania pulls hair in order to soothe his or her feelings, or to relieve boredom. Feelings about appearance do not motivate the pulling.[10]

The Biology of Trichotillomania

Studies of the brain chemistry behind trichotillomania have focused on understanding and controlling the repetitive nature of the hair pulling. Since unwanted repetitive actions are a major part of obsessive-compulsive disorder (OCD), some doctors have used medications for OCD to help people with trichotillomania. Many people with OCD have obtained relief from their compulsive behaviors by taking antidepressant medications that increase the amount of serotonin in the system. In addition to helping us control emotions and judgment, serotonin is the brain chemical most closely involved in starting and stopping behaviors, especially repetitive physical actions like pulling hair. However, those suffering from trichotillomania do not always receive the same benefit from these medications.[11]

One study of six people with both trichotillomania and either OCD or tics (involuntary muscle movements) found that they received no relief from hair pulling when they took medications that increased their levels of serotonin. However, the hair pulling decreased when they took dopamine-blocking medications.[12] The neurotransmitter dopamine, which controls feelings of pleasure, is also involved in regulating ritualized movements such as grooming activities.

Yet another neurochemical system, the opioid system, regulates the pleasure or pain a person feels when pulling hair. Neutralizing the effect of this neurotransmitter by means of an opioid blocking medication eliminates the pleasure from hair pulling. This has helped some people to stop.

Many different neurotransmitter systems appear to be involved in the occurrence and severity of trichotillomania. The interactions among the different neurotransmitters, rather than an abnormality in just one system, are probably the key factors.[13]

Trichotillomania in Animals

Cats, dogs, and birds share the human habit of pulling out feathers or licking their fur away when they are anxious. Two African grey parrots that picked their feathers had dramatic refeathering when given haloperidol, a drug that lowers the amount of dopamine in the brain. Cats and dogs that lick or scratch excessively have improved on similar medications.[14]

A slight tendency for trichotillomania to run in families has been observed, suggesting a genetic connection. However, children could simply be imitating the hair pulling behavior they see in adult members of their families. More research is needed in this area.[15]

Hair Pulling In Children

The number of young children pulling their hair out to a visible extent seems to be low, perhaps one percent of all children under the age of eight. But children as young as one year of age may pull their hair out. This is called "early-onset" hair pulling. The child usually pulls his or her hair in order to calm down. The pulling may occur when the child is tired, bored, or separated from a parent. Hair pulling may also become part of a bedtime ritual. In this way, hair pulling functions much like thumb sucking or rocking.[16] Young children do not seem to experience the "tension and relief" syndrome that affects many adults.[17]

Treatment

Parental awareness and help can usually allow a very young child to stop without outside treatment. However, a child over the age of eight may need professional assistance in stopping. The child's behavior may be a response to tension in the family. In this case, counseling for the whole family is indicated. Children and adolescents are usually not given medications for hair pulling, because of the unknown effect of psychiatric drugs on the developing brain.

Adolescents and adults benefit most from treatment that includes training in various strategies to change the hairpulling behavior. The most powerful behavioral technique for improving hairpulling behavior is habit reversal training. In this approach, the person learns to:

- identify the situations and actions that encourage hair pulling; and

- practice behaviors incompatible with hair pulling, such as fist clenching.

Support groups are very helpful for a disorder such as trichotillomania, because those who suffer from it usually feel embarrassed about their behavior and do not confide in anyone. The resulting sense of isolation can make the symptoms worse.[18]

Training in a relaxation technique, such as progressive muscle relaxation, can lower the amount of stress that many hair pullers feel as they try to give up their habit.

A variety of different antidepressants and anti-anxiety medications have been shown to lessen hair pulling behavior in certain individuals. However, there is no consistent pattern of relief with these medications. It is not uncommon for a person to see improvement for a short time and then a return to pulling hair when the effect of the medication ceases. But this brief period of improvement may encourage the trichotillomania sufferer to continue with other strategies that, over time, bring permanent lessening of the hair pulling.[19]

8

The Future and Impulse-Control Disorders

I mpulse-control disorders (ICDs) have only been identified in the *Diagnostic and Statistical Manual of Mental Disorders* since 1980. This period of time is too short to allow researchers to carry out the detailed investigation necessary to explain and find treatments for such complex disorders. Thus, our knowledge of impulse-control problems is still at a very early stage.

Several factors complicate the picture of impulse-control disorders. We do not yet have precise definitions of these disorders. We do not know exactly how they relate to other disorders and what role they play in a person's total personality. Researchers are still trying to work out the relationships among normal behavior, impulsivity, impulse-control disorders, and other psychological disorders.

We do know that a person suffering from an ICD almost always has at least one other psychological disorder. These other disorders can mask the existence or the severity of the ICD, making treatment of the ICD more difficult.

Many of the actions that define these disorders, such as stealing, setting fires, and violent outbursts, constitute illegal activities that can bring harm and even death to the perpetrator and others. People who engage in these actions may desperately want help, but they are afraid of what other people will think of them if they are found out. They do not want to be punished for actions that they cannot control.

However, impulsive acts with negative consequences are becoming more and more common in Western society. The rate of shoplifting is increasing. Road rage incidents appear almost daily in the newspapers. Arson is on the rise. The damaging effects of these kinds of impulsive behavior are obvious. What can be done to halt the negative effects of these actions on society, and help those who commit them to stop?

More and more incidents of road rage have begun appearing in the news.

More Research is Needed

The first step is studying each impulse-control disorder in greater detail. Researchers follow certain standard procedures in conducting such studies. Typically, they begin by gathering groups of people who appear to be experiencing the symptoms of the ICD being studied. The patients are interviewed and complete questionnaires to determine if they actually fit the DSM-IV criteria for the disorder. Those patients who meet the criteria are divided into groups, each of which receives a different treatment plan. The treatment may be medication, therapy, a combination of medication and therapy, or no treatment at all. The group that receives no treatment is called the control group. When the treatment is completed, usually after a period of months, the patients are interviewed again. The results of these interviews are compared with the first interviews. The comparisons reveal which types of treatment work best for the patients.

Research studies trying to pinpoint what these disorders are and which treatments work best have produced contradictory conclusions. Pathological gambling has been described as an impulse-control disorder, a compulsion, and an addiction. Kleptomania may be an expression of obsessive-compulsive disorder or depression. Trichotillomania is perhaps the biggest puzzle. Different studies have found it to be part of a personality disorder (a continuing pattern of negative interpersonal skills), body dysmorphic disorder (worrying about one's appearance), or a type of motor tic (uncontrollable repeated physical action). It has strong compulsive as well as impulsive elements.

Little research has been conducted on the remaining two impulse-control disorders, perhaps because they are so rare.

Results of the first study of intermittent explosive disorder, which included only 27 patients, were published in 1998 and 1999.[1] That study stated that IED might be related to bipolar disorder, in which a patient's moods swing from elation to deep depression. Pyromania is diagnosed so rarely that there are not enough patients to study. Information about pyromania comes mainly from studies of fire-setting behavior.

The Spectrum Model of Impulsive and Compulsive Behavior

Dr. Eric Hollander, director of the Compulsive, Impulsive, and Anxiety Disorders Program at the Mount Sinai School of Medicine in New York City, has been involved with a great deal of the research carried out so far on impulse-control disorders. Dr. Hollander feels that impulsive and compulsive actions are often related, and stem from the same psychological source. He suggests that they are a type of obsessive-compulsive disorder.

At first, the occurrence of impulsive and compulsive behaviors together seems strange. How can someone's behavior be both impulsive, meaning spontaneous, and at the same time compulsive, meaning controlled and forced? Dr. Hollander says that impulsive and compulsive behavior patterns share a common core: a lack of control over behavior caused by a person's emotions. People with impulsive disorders do not have enough control because they do not consider the results of their behavior. Those with compulsive disorders exert too much control because they are trying to avoid anxiety or fear. The two types of behavior fall at opposite ends of a spectrum of control. A person may behave more compulsively or more impulsively—in other words, shifting from one end of the control spectrum to the other—while still suffering from a single disorder.[2]

A good example of this overlap of impulsive and compulsive symptoms occurs in pathological gambling. A gambler often makes a spontaneous decision to gamble. However, many gamblers gamble repeatedly, and when they are not gambling they are thinking about when they will next gamble, or where to get the money to gamble, or reliving the last time they gambled. It is the combination of both impulsive and compulsive actions that makes up the disorder of pathological gambling.[3]

What is Obsessive-Compulsive Disorder?

A person with obsessive-compulsive disorder (OCD) constantly experiences upsetting thoughts that do not go away. The person develops stereotyped acts, called rituals, to try to control the thoughts. However, the thoughts keep popping up. Eventually, the thoughts and the rituals become associated in the person's mind, and the person suffers from both the upsetting thoughts and the ritual behavior.

Amy is a typical example of a teenager with OCD. Ever since she was a child, Amy had been afraid that something bad would happen to her family. Her worries became obsessive, meaning that she could not stop worrying even when she knew her family was perfectly all right. One day, she had an idea. If she did everything three times, maybe nothing bad would happen to her family. Amy started putting three ice cubes in her drinks, using the third piece of silverware from the drawer, and bouncing a volleyball three times before serving. Soon Amy did everything three times, no matter what the situation. What had started out as an impulse became a compulsion, something Amy felt she just had to do. Amy was not able to visit her friends because her bizarre behavior interfered with their activities. She was deeply ashamed but unable to stop her worrying or her ritual behavior. Amy was suffering from obsessive thoughts and compulsive behaviors.[4]

The Circumplex Theory

People with impulse-control disorders often suffer also from psychological disorders outside the impulsive-compulsive spectrum. Depression, anxiety, and substance abuse are the most common, but there are many others. When a person experiences more than one psychological disorder, the disorders are called co-occurring or co-morbid.

One theory of impulse-control disorders tries to take these co-morbid conditions into account. The circumplex theory states that patients frequently suffer from more than one psychological problem. The problems may occur in different degrees: mild, moderate, or severe. A doctor using this approach will list all the different disorders and note how severe they are. From this list, the doctor creates a profile that describes the whole person. This approach moves away from a focus on the disorders and encourages treatment of the person as a whole.[5]

For example, a man was admitted to a psychiatric hospital after he tried to kill himself. He told his doctor that he had lost his appetite and could not sleep. He felt sad, had trouble concentrating, and found himself crying for no reason. He also admitted that he had stolen things he did not need from work and stores for over ten years. He had been fired from several jobs because of stealing, which he said he did about twice a week. The doctor determined that the man suffered from two disorders: depression and kleptomania. He felt that the depression was more severe than the kleptomania. The patient received medication for depression but did not come in for counseling. Three months later, the patient was surprised to find that he was not only less depressed, he had actually stopped stealing.[6]

Brain Imaging Techniques

New research techniques are being developed to help us understand the biology behind impulse-control disorders. Several new imaging procedures allow scientists to study the structure of the brain in ways that the doctors who treated Phineas Gage could not even imagine.

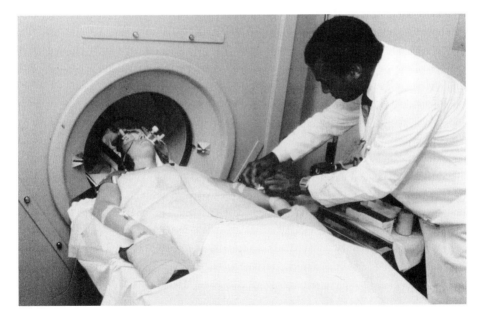

Positron Emission Tomography, or PET, is helpful in identifying the locations and intensity of brain activity.

Positron Emission Tomography (PET) uses nuclear particles called positrons to create pictures of blood flow and bodily functions in various organs. It is especially useful in identifying the locations and intensity of brain activity. A liquid containing positrons is injected into one of the patient's arteries, while a computer maps the flow of the liquid as it moves through blood vessels and tissues. Then the computer processes the data from the test and creates pictures of the activity.

Functional Magnetic Resonance Imaging (fMRI) uses the power of a large magnet to take pictures of the soft tissues inside the body. It can show the brain and other organs as they work, revealing which parts of an organ are active and which are not.

These techniques are providing more information about the role of the functioning and structure of the brain in impulse-control problems. For example, researchers have found that the volume of blood flow in the frontal lobes of the brains of people with various kinds of impulse-control disorders is sometimes lower than in the brains of people without such disorders. This suggests that decreased activity in this part of the brain may be at least partly responsible for lowered impulse control.[7]

Damage to or abnormalities in the limbic system have also been found in the brains of people with higher-than-average impulsivity. People with this kind of abnormality have a tendency to act aggressively.[8]

The Human Brain Project

Information about the brain from PET and fMRI scans, as well as from other sources, is rapidly building up. In order for this material to help us understand how the brain works, it must be made available to other researchers in an easy-to-use form.

This is not a simple task. Electronic brain scans create computerized three-dimensional, visual models of the brain. Each scan requires massive amounts of computer storage space. Furthermore, the different types of scans are set up differently. Finally, a complete understanding of the brain requires scientists to include DNA samples and information about the person's education, diet, and life experiences. How can all this different material be brought together?

The Human Brain Project began in 1993 as a way to make all the information about the brain available in a uniform computerized format. Today, it includes researchers from around the world. The $14 million project is funded by the National Institute of Mental Health and many other federal agencies. Other countries around the world are contributing up to $30 million to gather data on the brain. The development of computer storage and use of information from neuroscience is called neuroinformatics.[9]

At UCLA, a special computer, known as the Reality Monster, has been designed to hold the vast amount of information required to start understanding the three-pound organ each one of us has inside our skulls. The material necessary to describe just one brain occupies the computer space equivalent of one million books. When this piece of the Human Brain Project is complete, the Reality Monster will contain detailed information on 7,000 brains.[10]

Impulsive Behavior and the Law

At the present time, no foolproof treatment exists that enables a person to control his or her impulses all the time. This means that the legal system must become involved when impulsive actions result in harm.

Imagine a boy named Thomas. Thomas is in a courtroom standing before a judge, his head hanging down. Only twelve years old, he is appearing in court for the third time in a year. He has been caught setting a fire, again. The first two fires consumed some hay. This time, however, his neighbor's house burned to the ground. The occupants were lucky to escape with their lives.

Thomas tells the judge he could not stop himself. He does not even remember setting the fire. What sentence does Thomas receive? This depends on when in history Thomas committed his crime.

In England in the year 1300, Thomas would be treated according to the *lex talionis*. This Latin term expresses the concept of "vengeance in kind." In other words, he would be burned to death, just as he had burned someone or something else.

If Thomas were living in 1750, he could face death by hanging. Arson was a capital offense in England until the 1860s, meaning that it was punishable by death. Children as young as seven were tried as adults, if they showed intent to do harm. In actual practice, children were executed for crimes far less frequently than adults. But they did not get off scot-free. They were often sent to live in one of the distant British colonies, or forced to become sailors in the British navy.

In the United States in 2002, Thomas can expect a very different future. He must pay for the damage he caused, of course. He will probably be sent to a residential treatment facility for juvenile criminals. Food, education, and a warm bed will be provided for him, as well as counseling, until he appears able to stop setting fires. Then, he will be released.

When Is A Child A Child?

Twelve-year-old Lionel Tate admitted to killing the six-year-old child he was playing with on July 28, 1999. Lionel said he did not mean to hurt her. He was imitating professional wrestling moves he had seen on TV as they played. A Florida jury found him guilty of first-degree murder. He received the mandatory adult sentence of life in prison.

Many people were shocked at the harshness of the verdict. Even the lawyers who prosecuted Lionel said they would not have opposed a lesser sentence or clemency from the governor of Florida.[11]

Who Is Responsible?

Does this change in the way the criminal justice system handles young criminals mean we can now cure destructive habits like setting fires or compulsive gambling? Not at all. It reflects a change in society's attitude toward such actions. This change is very controversial.

Scientific research is beginning to uncover the biology behind impulsive behavior. It appears that a tendency toward impulsivity may be passed down through our chromosomes, just like our hair color or our height. We also are becoming aware of the powerful effect of upbringing and environment on behavior. Some fear that these discoveries will allow us to feel less responsible for our actions. Does saying that a woman suffers from kleptomania or that a man has a pathological gambling problem mean the people cannot, or do not have to, help themselves? Or do such labels

Boot Camp

Teenage criminals are sometimes sent to facilities that resemble military training camps rather than jails. Boys and girls sport shaved heads. Inmates must rise before dawn, scrub their quarters spotless, and participate in vigorous physical exercise. They also study the same subjects that they would in regular school. Television, radio, magazines, and newspapers are forbidden. Their 8:00 P.M. bedtime finds them exhausted.

Opinions are divided about the effectiveness of these harsh living situations. Some members of the public feel that a combination of stark living conditions, stern military training and no-nonsense educational basics will correct problem behavior by forcing the teens to grow up in a hurry. But others point out that over half of the teens who go through boot camp incarcerations will be arrested again.[12]

enable them to get the help they need?[13] As our knowledge of the causes of human behavior expands, we must ask ourselves who is responsible for our actions.

John J. Ratey, a well-known doctor who has written extensively on personality disorders and attention-deficit/hyperactivity disorder, proposes a positive way of integrating biological discoveries and social responsibility. He says that the new biology does not "release us from personal responsibility...our responsibility in this new era is to acknowledge our biology, understand our biology, and take whatever steps we need to take in order to prevent that biology from harming our lives or the lives of those we love."[14]

Impulse-Control Disorders At Work

These difficult questions about responsibility have moved into the workplace with the passage of the Americans with Disabilities Act (ADA) in 1990. The ADA provides protection for workers who have specified physical and/or mental handicaps. Employers cannot refuse to hire people with these conditions simply because of them. Employers must also make allowances to help disabled employees while they are working. Until now, pyromania, kleptomania, illegal drug use and sexual behavior disorders have been expressly excluded from the list of protected conditions. Some people wonder if the increasing tendency to classify antisocial behaviors as "disorders" will result in pyromania and other behaviors being considered as disabilities. Under this scenario, fire companies would be required to hire people with documented histories of fire setting, and stealing the company fax machine would be a protected activity for a kleptomaniac, not subject to prosecution.[15]

Q & A

Q. What causes impulse-control disorders (ICDs)?

A. No one knows for sure. The structure and chemistry of a person's brain, the way the person was brought up, and the person's environment all play roles in the development of impulsive behavior.

Q. Are impulse-control disorders real or just excuses for bad behavior?

A. There is disagreement on this topic. Although some people may use the label of an ICD to avoid taking responsibility for their actions, most people with these disorders desperately want to stop their destructive behavior.

Q. My uncle gambles all the time. His wife left him because he spent all their money. Will I turn out like him?

A. A tendency to gamble does appear to run in families. All the ICDs seem to be able to be inherited, in mild or strong forms. Being aware of this tendency can help you take steps right now, like avoiding opportunities to gamble and going to a support group, that will help you to avoid developing the habit of gambling.

Q. I used to pull my hair out when I was younger, but I stopped. Lately I have noticed that I am doing it again. What should I do?

A. Get help immediately, before the habit becomes too strong to stop. A counselor, therapist, or your doctor can advise you. You may benefit from medication as well as from behavioral therapy.

Q. My friend takes little things like socks and nail polish from stores all the time. She wants me to do the same thing. What should I tell her? I want to be her friend.

A. Do not follow in her footsteps. Tell her that stealing is illegal, no matter how inexpensive the item might be. Ask her how she will feel if she gets caught. You may need to avoid going shopping with your friend.

Q. I think I have a problem controlling my temper. I get mad all the time and I feel like doing damage. I do not want to tell anyone.

A. There are many on-line resources for you to find help. Check the Internet or the phone book for organizations that provide counseling for anger. Your doctor or minister can also make suggestions. People involved in counseling know how important confidentiality is. They will not tell anyone about your problem.

Q. My sister has wild mood swings every few days. Sometimes, she is so down she does not even want to go to school. Last week, she stayed up all night painting her room, then started in on the living room walls as well! What is wrong with her?

A. Your sister may be suffering from bipolar disorder. This is the name given to the pattern of up and down mood swings that you described. Professional counseling and possibly medications will help her.

Q. One night my brother drank a couple of beers when our parents were not home. He "accidentally" set fire to the garden shed. Was this really an accident?

A. Alcohol, drugs, and stress can cause a person to lose control over impulsive thoughts. It is important to know what factors cause a person to lose control, and avoid them. Your brother may be unhappy about something and not know how to express his feelings. He needs counseling for his feelings and about the dangers of fire.

Q. I feel like I have to do things a certain way every day. If I do not close my bedroom door five times before I go to bed, I am afraid someone will break into the house. Is this normal?

A. It may be a sign of obsessive-compulsive disorder (OCD). Trying to control a fear by repeated, ritual actions is typical of OCD. Ask your parents to take you to your doctor, and get counseling.

Impulse-Control Disorder Timeline

c. 2000 B.C.—Hebrew, Mesopotamian, Indian, and other ancient stories describe impulsive behavior such as intermittent violence and gambling.

c. 400 B.C.—Hippocrates attributes impulsive behavior to an excess of yellow bile in the body. He also notes hair pulling as an important medical symptom.

400-1600 A.D.—Impulsive behavior is regarded as the work of the devil and a sign of a bad character.

Early 1800s—Doctors note that damage to the frontal lobes of the brain results in impulsive behavior.

1801—Dr. Philippe Pinel describes impulsive behavior as an illness.

1838—The term *kleptomania* is coined in France by Drs. Étienne Esquirol and Charles Chrétien Marc.

1869—Dr. George Miller Beard writes a book on nervous exhaustion, an ailment that includes impulsivity.

1889—Dr. H. Hallopeau invents the term *trichotillomania* to describe repeated hair pulling.

Early 1900s—Dr. Sigmund Freud declares that impulses are neither good nor bad, and are something everyone feels.

1902—Dr. Ehrlheim Hirt publishes the first textbook that includes a clinically accurate description of impulsive behavior.

1914—Doctors notice that children in a British orphanage pull their hair out in response to stress.

1980—Four impulse control disorders—pyromania, kleptomania, intermittent rage disorder, and pathological gambling—are included in the *Diagnostic and Statistical Manual of Mental Disorders*, Third Edition.

1987—Trichotillomania is added to the revised Third Edition of the *DSM*.

1994—The Fourth Edition of the *DSM* appears, containing all five impulse-control disorders.

Glossary

Americans with Disabilities Act (ADA)—A package of laws, passed in 1990, that protects workers with physical and mental handicaps.

antidepressant medications—Medications that regulate the availability and absorption of neurotransmitters in the brain.

arson—The deliberate setting of a fire.

behavioral therapy—A psychological treatment focusing on a person's behavior and how to control it.

bipolar disorder—Also called manic depression, it involves repeated mood swings, from very excited to deeply depressed.

body dysmorphic disorder (BDD)—Worrying excessively about a real or imagined defect in a person's appearance.

cerebellum—The part of the brain that controls movement and coordination.

cerebrum—The largest part of the human brain. It houses language abilities, abstract thinking, and control of impulses.

chromosomes—Biological codes for basic physical and mental characteristics, found in body cells.

cognitive therapy—A psychological treatment that identifies negative thought patterns and helps a person "rethink" more positively.

Diagnostic and Statistical Manual of Mental Disorders (DSM)—A catalog of all known mental and psychological disorders. Now in its fourth edition (*DSM-IV-TR*).

dopamine—A brain chemical associated with feelings of excitement and pleasure.

firesetter—A person who sets fires for reasons not related to the usual uses of fire.

frontal lobes—The part of the cerebrum thought to be most involved in the regulation of impulses.

habit reversal training—A psychological treatment that substitutes a less harmful action for one that causes the person distress.

impulse—A sudden feeling or urge to act that arises from inside a person's mind.

impulse control disorder (ICD)—Repeated impulsive actions that result in negative consequences.

impulsivity—The habit of acting without thinking more often than most people.

intermittent explosive disorder (IED)—Episodic loss of control resulting in physical violence.

kleptomania—Stealing things that a person does not need.

lex talionis—Latin term meaning "vengeance in kind."

limbic system—The part of the brain that generates basic emotions and impulses.

neurasthenia—A term popular in the mid-nineteenth century, meaning nervous exhaustion.

neurons—Brain cells that transmit feelings and information.

neurotransmitter—A brain chemical that passes information from one neuron to another.

noradrenalin—A brain chemical that stimulates the nervous system and releases energy in the body.

obsessive-compulsive disorder (OCD)—A pattern of troubling thoughts and stereotyped behavior that is believed to control the thoughts.

opioid system—Brain chemicals involved in perceptions of pleasure and pain.

pathological gambling—Uncontrollable gambling that results in the loss of large sums of money.

pyromania—Setting fires for pleasure or to obtain relief from strong emotions.

remission—A period of time when the behavior of an impulse-control disorder stops.

serotonin—A brain chemical involved in emotions, feelings, and judgment.

shoplifting—Taking something from a store without paying.

social gambling—Gambling with friends, for a limited time, with a preset dollar limit.

synapse—The space between two brain cells.

trichotillomania—Pulling hair out as a way to relax or to avoid boredom.

For More Information

American Burn Association
http://www.ameriburn.org

Debtors Anonymous
P.O. Box 920888
Needham, MA 02492-0009
(781) 453-2743
http://www.debtorsanonymous.org

Gamblers Anonymous
P.O. Box 17173
Los Angeles, CA 90017
(213) 386-8789
http://www.gamblersanonymous.org

National Center for
   Responsible Gaming
P. O. Box 25366
Kansas City, MO 64119-0666
(816) 453-9964
http://www.ncrg.org

National Council on Problem
   Gambling
1-800-522-4700
http://www.ncpgambling.org

Obsessive-Compulsive Foundation
337 Notch Hill Road
North Branford, CT 06471
(203) 315-2190
http://www.ocfoundation.org

Obsessive-Compulsive Information
   Center
7617 Mineral Point Road, Suite 300
Madison, WI 53717
(608) 827-2470
http://www.healthtechsys.com

Obsessive-Compulsive Resource Center
http://www.ocdresource.com

Shoplifters Alternative
380 N. Broadway
Jericho, NY 11753
(888) 466-2299
http://www.shopliftersalternative.org

National Trichotillomania Learning
   Center
1215 Mission St., Suite 2
Santa Cruz, CA 95060
(831) 457-1004
http://www.trich.org

Chapter Notes

Chapter 1. What Are Impulse-Control Disorders?

1. Richard Jerome, "Disarming the Rage," *People,* June 4, 2001, pp. 60–61.

2. "The Strangest Obsession of All," *Ladies' Home Journal,* March 1993, pp. 106–108, 113.

3. Scott J. Dickman, "Impulsivity and Information Processing," *The Impulsive Client: Theory, Research, and Treatment,* ed. William G. McCown, et al. (Washington, D.C.: American Psychological Association, 1993) p. 151.

4. Mollie Keller, *Marie Curie* (New York: Franklin Watts, 1982), p. 115.

5. William G. McCown and Philip A. DeSimone, "Impulses, Impulsivity, and Impulsive Behaviors: A Historical Review of a Contemporary Issue," *The Impulsive Client: Theory, Research, and Treatment,* ed. William G. McCown, et al. (Washington, D.C.: American Psychological Association, 1993) pp. 3–4.

6. R. Plutchik and H. M. Van Praag, "Interrelations Among Anxiety, Depression, Aggression, Impulsivity and Suicidality: An Evaluation of the Comorbidity Concept," in *Neurobiology and Clinical Views on Aggression and Impulsivity,* ed. Michael Maes and Emil F. Coccaro (New York: John Wiley and Sons, Ltd., 1998), p. 2.

7. John Evenden, "Impulsivity: A Discussion of Clinical and Experimental Findings," *Journal of Psychopharmacology,* Volume 13, Number 2, 1999, p. 188.

8. H. Spencer Bloch, *Adolescent Development, Psychopathology, and Treatment* (Madison, Conn.: International Universities Press, Inc., 1995), p. 311.

9. American Psychiatric Association, *Diagnostic and Statistical Manual of Mental Disorders, Fourth Edition Text Revision* (Washington, D.C.: American Psychiatric Association, 2000), pp. 668, 673, 676.

10. James Morgan, "What Makes Kleptomaniacs Steal?" *Health,* September 1997, p. 104.

11. Eric Hollander, Alison Buchalter, and Concetta M. DeCaria, "Pathological Gambling," *The Psychiatric Clinics of North America,* September 2000, p. 630.

12. Eric Hollander and J. Rosen, "Impulsivity," *Journal of Psychopharmacology,* Volume 14, Number 2, Supplement 1, 2000, p. 39.

Chapter 2. History, Causes, and Treatment of Impulse-Control Disorders

1. William G. McCown and Philip A. DeSimone, "Impulses, Impulsivity, and Impulsive Behaviors: a Historical Review of a Contemporary Issue," *The Impulsive Client: Theory, Research, and Treatment,* ed. William G. McCown, et al. (Washington, D.C.: American Psychological Association, 1993), pp. 6–10.

2. Anson Rabinbach, *The Human Motor* (New York: Basic Books, 1990), pp. 153–155.

3. McCown and DeSimone, pp. 10–19.

4. Hanna Damasio, et al., "The Return of Phineas Gage: Clues About the Brain from the Skull of a Famous Patient," *Science,* May 20, 1994, p. 1102.

5. Diana Fishbein, "Neuropsychological Function, Drug Abuse, and Violence," *Criminal Justice and Behavior,* April 2000, p. 142.

6. John Evenden, "Impulsivity: A Discussion of Clinical and Experimental Findings," *Journal of Psychopharmacology,* Volume 13, Number 2, 1999, p. 187.

7. R. Plutchik and H. M. Van Praag, "Interrelations Among Anxiety, Depression, Aggression, Impulsivity and Suicidality: An Evaluation of the Comorbidity Concept," in *Neurobiology and Clinical Views on Aggression and Impulsivity,* ed. Michael Maes and Emil F. Coccaro (New York: John Wiley and Sons, 1998), pp. 5–7.

8. Richard J. Kavoussi and Emil F. Coccaro, "Biology and Pharmacological Treatment of Impulse-Control Disorders," in *Impulsivity and Compulsivity,* ed. John M. Oldham, et al. (Washington, D.C.: American Psychiatric Press, 1996), pp. 134–135.

9. C. S. Bergeman and A. D. Seroczynski, "Genetic and Environmental Influences on Aggression and Impulsivity," in *Neurobiology and Clinical Views on Aggression and Impulsivity,* ed. Michael Maes and Emil F. Coccaro (New York: John Wiley and Sons, 1998), p. 65.

10. Jasmine A. Tehrani and Sarnoff A. Mednick, "Genetic Factors and Criminal Behavior," *Federal Probation,* December 2000, pp. 24–27.

11. Aileen D. Fink and William G. McCown, "Impulsivity in Children and Adolescents: Measurement, Causes, and Treatment," in *The Impulsive Client: Theory, Research, and Treatment*, ed. William G. McCown, et al. (Washington, D.C.: American Psychological Association, 1993), p. 297.

12. Russell Barkley, et al., "Multi-Method Psycho-Educational Intervention for Preschool Children with Disruptive Behavior: Preliminary Results at Post-Treatment," *Journal of Child Psychology and Psychiatry*, March 2000, pp. 319–332.

13. Kavoussi and Coccaro, pp. 125–130.

Chapter 3. Pyromania

1. George A. Sakheim and Elizabeth Osborn, "Severe vs. Nonsevere Firesetters Revisited," *Child Welfare*, July/August 1999, pp. 413–415.

2. American Psychiatric Association, *Diagnostic and Statistical Manual of Mental Disorders*, Fourth Edition Text Revision (Washington, D.C.: American Psychiatric Association, 2000), p. 671.

3. Ellen Emerson White, "Profiling Arsonists and their Motives: An Update," *Fire Engineering*, March 1996, p. 84.

4. The information in this section comes from: Phil Boyle, "Children Who Commit Arson Are Topic of Burn Prevention Session," *The Morning Call*, Allentown, Penn., March 28, 2001, sec.B, p. 2; Michael L. Slavkin and Kenneth Fineman, "What Every Professional Who Works With Adolescents Needs to Know About Firesetters," *Adolescence*, Winter 2000, p. 759.

5. Sakheim and Osborn, p. 413.

6. The information in this section comes from: White; Boyle; Federal Bureau of Investigation, "Crime in the United States, 1999," Press Release, October 15, 2000.

7. "Hot Tots," *Psychology Today*, March/April 1996, p. 11.

8. Sakheim and Osborn, p. 415; and Lynn A. Stewart, "Profiles of Female Firesetters," *British Journal of Psychiatry*, Volume 163, 1993, p. 254.

9. Grant T. Harris and Marnie E. Rice, "A Typology of Mentally Disordered Firesetters," *Journal of Interpersonal Violence*, September 1996, p. 351.

10. Unless otherwise noted, information in this section comes from: White, pp. 80–82.

11. "Sacked Worker Sought for Arson Attack on Store," *Hong Kong Mail,* March 9, 2001.

12. "Arsonists Stage Triple Attack to 'Avenge' Boy's Death," *AP Worldstream,* March 8, 2001.

13. Sakheim and Osborn, pp. 427–428.

14. "Mom Allegedly Set Fires to Help Firefighter Son," *The Morning Call,* August 5, 1995, sec. A, p. 17.

15. George Sakheim, et al., "Toward a Clearer Differentiation of High-Risk from Low-Risk Fire-Setters," *Child Welfare,* July–August 1991, pp. 409–502.

16. Kendall Hamilton and Marc Peyser, "Cartoon Culprits?" *Newsweek,* October 18, 1993, p. 10.

17. "Hot Tots," *Psychology Today.*

18. Boyle.

Chapter 4. Kleptomania

1. Gennifer Dixon (not her real name) as told to Stephanie Booth, "I Got Caught Shoplifting," *Teen,* September 1999, p. 89.

2. The information in this section comes from: Marcus J. Goldman, *Kleptomania* (Far Hills, N.J.: New Horizon Press, 1998), pp. xiii, 52; James Morgan, "What Makes Kleptomaniacs Steal?" *Health,* September 1997, p. 104; Read Hayes, "Tailoring Security to Fit the Criminal," *Security Management,* July 1999, p. 116; Jack Ford, Connie Chung, and Sylvia Chase, "The Queen of Shoplifting," ABC Nightline transcript, October 4, 1999, unpaged.

3. Joseph Altman, Jr., "Three Shoplifting Suspects Killed In Year in Detroit," *The Morning Call* (Allentown, Penn.), April 7, 2001, sec. A, p. 24.

4. Morgan, pp. 105–106.

5. Larry Kanter, "Tabletop Thieves," *Crain's New York Business,* November 15, 1999, pp. 3–4.

6. Hayes, p. 116.

7. Goldman, p. 52.

8. Ibid., pp. 51–52.

9. Morgan, p. 104.

10. American Psychiatric Association, *Diagnostic and Statistical Manual of Mental Disorders*, Fourth Edition Text Revision (Washington, D.C.: American Psychiatric Association, 2000), p. 669.

11. St. Augustine, *Confessions*, Book 2, Chapter 4. Translated by the author.

12. Goldman, pp. 9, 57, 85.

13. Larry K. Brown, "Petticoat Prisoners of Old Wyoming," *Wild West*, February 1998, p. 54.

14. Goldman, pp. 170–187.

15. John E. Kraus, "Treatment of Kleptomania with Paroxetine," *Journal of Clinical Psychiatry*, November 1999, p. 793.

16. Goldman, p. 183.

17. Richard Chin, "Drugs May Submerge Urge to Steal," *Saint Paul Pioneer Press*, St. Paul, Minn., December 6, 2000, unpaged.

18. Ford, Chung, and Chase.

19. Lauren Coleman-Lochner, "Compulsive Shopping Viewed By Some as Medical, Genetic Disorder," *The Record*, April 5, 2000, unpaged.

20. Ronald J. Faber, "Money Changes Everything," *American Behavioral Scientist*, July/August 1992, p. 810.

Chapter 5. Pathological Gambling

1. Mark Rafenstein, "Why Teens are Becoming Compulsive about Gambling," *Current Health* 2, April/May 2000, pp. 26–28.

2. American Psychiatric Association, *Diagnostic and Statistical Manual of Mental Disorders*, Fourth Edition Text Revision (Washington, D.C.: American Psychiatric Association, 2000), pp. 671–674.

3. Richard J. Kavoussi and Emil F. Coccaro, "Biology and Pharmacological Treatment of Impulse-Control Disorders," in *Impulsivity and Compulsivity*, ed. John M. Oldham, et al. (Washington, D.C.: American Psychiatric Press, 1996), pp. 124–125.

4. Eric Hollander and J. Rosen, "Impulsivity," *Journal of Psychopharmacology*, Volume 14, Number 2, Supplement 1, p. S40.

5. D. W. Black and T. Moyer, "Clinical Features and Psychiatric Comorbidity of Subjects With Pathological Gambling Behavior," *Psychiatric Services*, Volume 49, 1998, pp. 1434–1439.

6. Nancy Mades, "Uneducated Risk," http://www.additudemag.com. (May 3, 2002).

7. Eric Hollander, Alison Buchalter, and Concetta M. DeCaria, "Pathological Gambling," *The Psychiatric Clinics of North America*, September 2000, p. 631.

8. Zachary Steel and Alex Blaszczynski, "Impulsivity, Personality Disorders and Pathological Gambling Severity," *Addiction*, Volume 93, Number 6, 1998, p. 896.

9. Carole J. Makela, "Youth Gambling: A Consumer Issue," *Consumer Interests Annual*, Issue 46, 2000, p. 218.

10. Rachel A. Volberg, "The Future of Gambling in the United Kingdom," *British Medical Journal*, June 10, 2000, p. 1556.

11. Barbara Sibbald, "Casinos Bring Ill Fortune, Psychiatrists Warn," *Canadian Medical Association Journal*, February 6, 2001, p. 388.

12. Dave Palermo, "Youth Getting Early Start May Face Problems With Gambling, Researchers Say," *The Sun Herald*, Biloxi, Miss., December 8, 2000, unpaged.

13. James R. Westphal, et al., "Gambling Behavior of Louisiana Students in Grades 6 Through 12," *Psychiatric Services*, January 2000, pp. 96–99.

14. Roy Porter, *English Society in the Eighteenth Century* (New York: Penguin Books, 1982), pp. 254–256.

15. Timothy A. Kelly, "A Booming $800 Billion Industry," *The World and I*, July 2000, p. 34.

16. Laurence Arnold, "Military Runs Overseas Slot Machines," *Associated Press Online*, January 13, 2001, unpaged.

17. Kelly, p. 37.

18. Hollander, et al., pp. 634–635.

19. David C. Hodgins and Nady El-Guebaly, "Natural and Treatment-Assisted Recovery From Gambling Problems: A Comparison of Resolved and Active Gamblers," *Addiction*, Volume 95, Number 5, 2000, p. 787.

20. Sharing Recovery Through Gamblers Anonymous (Los Angeles: Anonymous Publishing, Inc., 1984), p. 8.

21. Palermo.

Chapter 6. Intermittent Explosive Disorder

1. Donna De La Cruz, "8-Year-Old Faces Homicide Charge in Death of Boy, 4," *The Morning Call* (Allentown, Penn.), September 8, 2001, p. A-32.

2. "How To Keep Anger Under Control," *Jet,* June 1, 1998, pp. 54–57.

3. "Violence and Mental Health—Part I," *The Harvard Mental Health Letter,* January 2000, p. 1.

4. "Recidivism, Executive Summary," http://www.dc.state.fl.us/pub/recidivism/exec.html, unpaged (May 3,2002).

5. Julie Sevrens, "Experts Wonder If Society Isn't Boiling Over With Anger," *San Jose Mercury News,* San Jose, Calif., July 28, 2000, unpaged.

6. Bill Hewitt, "Collared," *People,* April 30, 2001, pp. 48–51.

7. Ron Harris, "Road-Rage Dog-Killer Gets 3 Years," *The Morning Call,* July 14, 2001, sec. A, p. 19.

8. Nayab Chohan, "Three Held for US 'air rage'," *The Times,* London, England, May 21, 2001, unpaged.

9. Sevrens.

10. John Harlow, "Naomi Punches Out Her Anger," *The Sunday Times,* London, England, November 19, 2000, News Section, p. 7 (for Tyson); Jonathan Sackier and John Morgan, "Anger Can Be Hazardous to Your Health, " http://www.usatoday.com/life/health/doctor/phdoc070.htm" January 14, 2000, unpaged (for Combs); Mike Conklin, "The Air is Rife with Hostility and Anger," Chicago Tribune, August 18, 2000, unpaged (for Knight and Eminem).

11. Timothy Hughes, "Shannen Doherty Is Arrested in DUI Case," *Los Angeles Times,* December 29, 2000, sec. B, p. 13.

12. Sevrens.

13. Conklin.

14. American Psychiatric Association, *Diagnostic and Statistical Manual of Mental Disorders,* Fourth Edition Text Revision (Washington, D.C.: American Psychiatric Association, 2000), p. 667.

15. Dana Knight, "Ernst and Young's New Center in Indianapolis Puts Emphasis on Relaxation," *The Indianapolis Star,* November 16, 2000, unpaged.

16. John J. Ratey and Catherine Johnson, *Shadow Syndromes* (New York: Pantheon Books, 1997), p. 149.

17. Andrew E. Skodol and John M. Oldham, "Phenomenology, Differential Diagnosis, and Comorbidity of the Impulsive-Compulsive Spectrum of Disorders," in *Impulsivity and Compulsivity,* ed. John M. Oldham, et al. (Washington, D.C.: American Psychiatric Press, 1996), p. 17.

18. "Man, 100, Cleared of Pouring Gas on Girlfriend, 38," *The Morning Call,* Allentown, Penn., sec. A, p. 27.

19. Ronny Frishman, "The Lost Boys," *Ladies Home Journal,* January 1995, pp. 76, 78, 85, 151.

20. Richard J. Kavoussi and Emil F. Coccaro, "Biology and Pharmacological Treatment of Impulse-Control Disorders," in *Impulsivity and Compulsivity,* ed. John M. Oldham, et al. (Washington, D.C.: American Psychiatric Press, 1996), p. 120.

21. Susan L. McElroy, et al., "DSM-IV Intermittent Explosive Disorder: A Report of 27 Cases," *Journal of Clinical Psychiatry,* April 1998, pp. 203–211.

22. James Chandler, "Bipolar Affective Disorder (Manic Depressive Disorder) in Children and Adults," www.klis.com/chandler/pamphlet/bipolar/bipolarpamphlet.htm (May 3,2002).

23. Ratey and Johnson, pp. 168–169.

24. "Controlling Anger—Before It Controls You," APA Online, unpaged.

25. "How To Keep Anger Under Control."

26. Sackier and Morgan.

27. John Cloud, "Classroom For Hotheads," *Time,* April 10, 2000, pp. 53–54.

Chapter 7. Trichotillomania

1. Karen A. Davis, "Appeals Court: Let Jury Decide Obsessive Primping Case," *The Morning Call* (Allentown, Penn.), March 24, 2001, sec. A, p. 26.

2. Gary A. Christenson and Charles S. Mansueto, "Trichotillomania: Descriptive Characteristics and Phenomenology," in *Trichotillomania,* ed. Dan J. Stein, et al. (Washington, D.C.: American Psychiatric Press, 1999), pp. 5–7.

3. American Psychiatric Association, *Diagnostic and Statistical Manual of Mental Disorders,* Fourth Edition Text Revision (Washington, D.C.: American Psychiatric Association, 2000), p. 677.

4. Christenson and Mansueto, pp. 10–20.

5. Richard L. O'Sullivan, Gary A. Christenson, and Dan J. Stein, "Pharmacotherapy of Trichotillomania," in *Trichotillomania,* ed. Dan J. Stein, et al. (Washington, D.C.: American Psychiatric Press, 1999), p. 105.

6. Haldin Davis, "Epidemic Alopecia Areata," *The British Journal of Dermatology*, June 1914, pp. 207–210.

7. Christenson and Mansueto, pp. 15–18.

8. Rachael Combe, "Excuse Me, Your Nervous Habit Is Showing," *Good Housekeeping*, August 1998, pp. 106–107.

9. Isaac Guzman, "Spotlight on the Backstreet Boys," *The Morning Call* (Allentown, Penn.), November 25, 2000, sec. A, pp. 31, 44.

10. Katharine A. Phillips, *The Broken Mirror—Understanding and Treating Body Dysmorphic Disorder* (New York: Oxford University Press, 1998), p. 53.

11. Suzan M. Streichenwein and Jack I. Thornby, "A Long-Term, Double-Blind, Placebo-Controlled Crossover Trial of the Efficacy of Fluoxetine for Trichotillomania," *American Journal of Psychiatry*, August 1995, p. 1196.

12. O'Sullivan, Christenson, and Stein, pp. 106–107.

13. Dan J. Stein, et al., "The Neurobiology of Trichotillomania," in *Trichotillomania*, ed. Dan J. Stein, et al. (Washington, D.C.: American Psychiatric Press, 1999), p. 49.

14. Alice A. Moon-Fanelli, et al., "Veterinary Models of Compulsive Self-Grooming: Parallels With Trichotillomania," in *Trichotillomania*, ed. Dan J. Stein, et al. (Washington, D.C.: American Psychiatric Press, 1999), pp. 73–82.

15. Christenson and Mansueto, pp. 32–33.

16. Richard O'Sullivan, et al., "Trichotillomania: Behavioral Symptom or Clinical Syndrome?" *American Journal of Psychiatry*, October 1997, p. 1445.

17. Elizabeth Reeve, "Hair Pulling in Children and Adolescents," in *Trichotillomania*, ed. Dan J. Stein, et al. (Washington, D.C.: American Psychiatric Press, 1999), p. 202.

18. O'Sullivan, et al., pp. 1445–1447.

19. O'Sullivan, Christenson, and Stein, p. 113.

Chapter 8. The Future and Impulse-Control Disorders

1. Susan L. McElroy, et al., "DSM-IV Intermittent Explosive Disorder: A Report of 27 Cases," *Journal of Clinical Psychiatry*, April 1998, pp. 203–211; and Susan L. McElroy, "Recognition and Treatment of DSM-IV Intermittent Explosive Disorder," *Journal of Clinical Psychiatry*, 1999, Volume 60, Supplement 15, pp. 12–16.

2. Andrew E. Skodol and John M. Oldham, "Phenomenology, Differential Diagnosis, and Comorbidity of the Impulsive-Compulsive Spectrum of Disorders," in *Impulsivity and Compulsivity*, ed. John M. Oldham, et al. (Washington, D.C.: American Psychiatric Press, 1996), pp. 2–3.

3. *Impulsivity and Compulsivity*, ed. John M. Oldham, et al. (Washington, D.C.: American Psychiatric Press, 1996), p. x.

4. Amy George (not her real name) as told to Sandy Fertman, "Secret Rituals, OCD, Obsessive-Compulsive Disorder, a Life Out of Control," *Teen*, July 2000, pp. 82–84.

5. R. Plutchik and H. M. Van Praag, "Interrelations Among Anxiety, Depression, Aggression, Impulsivity and Suicidality: An Evaluation of the Comorbidity Concept," in *Neurobiology and Clinical Views on Aggression and Impulsivity*, ed. Michael Maes, pp. 116–117.

6. John E. Kraus, "Treatment of Kleptomania with Paroxetine," Journal of Clinical Psychiatry, November 1999, p. 793.

7. Eric Hollander and Lisa J. Cohen, "Psychobiology and Psychopharmacology of Compulsive Spectrum Disorders," in *Impulsivity and Compulsivity*, ed. John M. Oldham, et al. (Washington, D.C.: American Psychiatric Press, 1996), pp. 148–150.

8. Dan J. Stein, et al., *Trichotillomania* (Washington, D.C.: American Psychiatric Press, 1999), pp. 96–97.

9. Robert Lee Hotz, "Byte by Byte, a Map of the Brain," *Los Angeles Times*, July 2, 2001, p. A–12.

10. Web site for the Human Brain Project: http://www.nimh.nih.gov/neuroinformatics/index.cfm.

11. "Defense to Appeal Boy's Murder Conviction in 'Wrestling Death'," CNN.com.law center, January 26, 2001; and "Wrestling Death Boy Moved to Juvenile Facility," *CNN.com.law center*, March 13, 2001.

12. Jessie Milligan, "Boot Camp is Popular in Concept, but Short on Effectiveness," *Fort Worth Star-Telegram*, Fort Worth, Texas, March 27, 2001, unpaged.

13. Bruce Wiseman, "Confronting the Breakdown of Law and Order," *USA Today* Magazine, January 1997, Volume 125, Issue 2660, pp. 32–34.

14. John R. Ratey and Catherine Johnson, *Shadow Syndromes* (New York: Pantheon Books, 1997), p. 19.

15. Dan Crawford, "Is Theft a Crime? Nope, Call It Disability," *Business First—Columbus*, July 25, 1997, pp. 13–14.

Further Reading

Books

Castellani, Brian. Pathological Gambling: *The Making of a Medical Problem.* Albany, NY: State University of New York Press, 2000.

Gilligan, James. *Violence: Reflections on a National Epidemic.* New York: Vintage Books, 1997.

Goldman, Marcus J. *Kleptomania.* Far Hills, N.J.: New Horizon Press, 1998.

Greenwood-Robinson, Maggie. *Hair Savers for Women—A Complete Guide to Preventing and Treating Hair Loss.* New York: Three Rivers Press, 2000.

Humphrey, Hale. *This Must Be Hell: A Look at Pathological Gambling.* New York: Universe.com, 2000.

Knapp, Brian. *Fire.* Austin, Texas: Steck Vaughn Library, 1990.

Licata, Renora. *Everything You Need to Know About Anger.* New York: Rosen Publishing Group, 1992.

Nichoff, Debra. *The Biology of Violence.* New York: Free Press, 1999.

Greene, Ross W. *The Explosive Child.* New York: HarperCollins, 1998.

Internet Addresses

Psychology Information Online
Internet resource for information on impulse-control disorders.
<http://www.psychologyinfo.com/problems/impulse_control.html>

Wanna Bet?
An online magazine for kids who are concerned about gambling addictions.
<http://www.wannabet.org>

Index